P9-CMS-997

THE REFERENCE SHELF VOLUME 46 NUMBER 3

REPRESENTATIVE AMERICAN SPEECHES: 1973-1974

EDITED BY WALDO W. BRADEN

Boyd Professor of Speech
Louisiana State University

THE H. W. WILSON COMPANY
NEW YORK 1974

THE REFERENCE SHELF

The books in this series contain reprints of articles, excerpts from books, and addresses on current issues and social trends in the United States and other countries. There are six separately bound numbers in each volume, all of which are generally published in the same calendar year. One number is a collection of recent speeches; each of the others is devoted to a single subject and gives background information and discussion from various points of view, concluding with a comprehensive bibliography. Books in the series may be purchased individually or on subscription.

REPRESENTATIVE AMERICAN SPEECHES: 1973-1974

International Standard Book Number 0-8242-0524-3

Library of Congress Catalog Card Number (38-27962)

PRINTED IN THE UNITED STATES OF AMERICA

PREFACE

AN OVERVIEW OF PUBLIC ADDRESS, 1973–1974

An open society struggles to carry on its business through a free exchange of ideas, arguments, and sentiments. During almost any week in any community in the United States, public discourse takes many forms, including dialogues, discussions, forums, interviews (on and off radio and television), lectures, sermons, sales pitches, and judicial forensics. Among the audiences addressed by the speakers in this volume are a church congregation, the Senate Foreign Relations Committee, the Yale Political Union, the New York Academy of Sciences, a general session of the national convention of the Speech Communication Association, the United States Senate, and a luncheon of the Association of Buying Offices, as well as various university gatherings.

Like a menacing dark storm, the agony of Watergate dominated the American scene this past year. As the months passed, tension continued to build, and the scandals in Washington increasingly filled the conversations and speeches of Americans. The hearings of the Senate Select Committee on Presidential Campaign Activities, televised from May 17 through August 12, brought thousands of viewers to their sets like the addictive daytime soap operas. With each session the tempo intensified as witnesses faced the probing and searching questions of the seven Senators and their assistants. The questioners pressed forward to unravel the threads of conspiracy, to find new evidence, to expose inconsistencies, and to synthesize their findings. Those called to testify struggled to limit the interrogatories, to respond without incrimination, to avoid entrapment, and, above all, to appear calm throughout the grueling sessions. The verbal exchanges between John J. Wilson, the lawyer representing former presidential aides John D. Erlichman and H. R. Haldeman, and the committee members added excitement to the proceedings. Occasional careless outbursts—such as the one by Democratic Senator Daniel K. Inouye of Hawaii, who, thinking his microphone was off, was heard to say of Ehrlichman, "What a liar," and Wilson's later reference to Inouye as "that little Jap"—detracted from the dignity of the probe and brought rebuttals in other places. (See speeches by Senator Lloyd M. Bentsen, Jr., of Texas, Senator James B. Allen of Alabama, and Representative Spark M. Matsunaga of Hawaii, *Congressional Record,* August 2, 1973.)

The unfolding of the Watergate investigations dictated the nature of President Nixon's public speaking. He countered new developments in the probes with speeches or press conferences. After remaining silent during the Senate committee's public hearings (twelve weeks and two million words), on August 15 the President preempted time on the three TV networks to make a major thirty-minute address which turned out to be "a reiteration of previous general denials . . . devoid of emotionalism and polemics that many have come to expect of a Richard Nixon under fire" (John Herbers, New York *Times,* August 19, 1973). According to the *National Observer,* he sought to leave "the impression of an interested, helpful spectator who wanted to do his share" (James R. Dickenson, August 25, 1973). Soon thereafter he spoke to the Veterans of Foreign Wars at their convention in New Orleans, becoming more direct, confident, and aggressive. Two days later, at his home in San Clemente, California, he took on reporters in full view of the cameras in an open-air, fifty-minute, give-and-take press conference, his first in five months.

The State of the Union Message, on January 30, 1974, was the President's first important speech of the new year. Presenting his policies to a joint session of the House and Senate and to the citizenry via television, he once more sought to rally public support. "Most of the Republicans stood and applauded while Democrats remained seated and silent," reported the *Wall Street Journal* (January 31, 1974). One critic called the speech an "old-fashioned political speech, emphasizing peace and prosperity, reassuring the country that it never had it so good, but would soon have it better" (New York *Times,* February 1, 1974). The following night, Mike Mansfield (Democrat, Montana), the majority leader in the Senate, issued a terse reply to the President, defending the Democratic party's positions on key issues.

Emphasizing his determination not to resign in order to forestall possible impeachment, Nixon followed with yet more personal appearances. But the pressure on him continued to increase, especially when the House, on February 6, by a vote of 410 to 4, gave broad powers of inquiry to its Judiciary Committee so that it could study the question of impeachment. The President's speechmaking, however, went on. He made a brief speech at the Lincoln Memorial on February 12 and followed it, on February 17, with a longer, supposedly nonpartisan, speech at the Honor the American Day celebration at Huntsville, Alabama. (This latter one was his first speaking appearance away from Washington since August 1973.)

The President faced press conferences on February 25, March 6 (a portion is reprinted in this volume), and March 15, and initiated a question-and-answer session with the press in Houston, Texas, at the convention of the National Association of Broadcasters on March 19. It was also in late March and April that the President began to be accused of playing "impeachment politics," the implication being that he was shaping his policies and programs in order to stimulate enough support among conservative politicians to stave off any vote of impeachment in the House and conviction in the Senate. Nixon also ventured into Michigan's Eighth Congressional District, on April 10, to campaign for a Republican candidate in a special election that was called to fill a vacant House seat. But the candidate lost and debate began anew over the President's worth as an ally to any Republican office seeker.

When the deadline to answer the subpoenas of the Judiciary Committee and the Justice Department approached in late April, the President made one of his boldest moves yet, for on the night of April 28 he delivered his most important address of the year and perhaps of his career. He announced the release of 1,254 pages and 200,000 words of edited transcripts of White House tapes relevant to Watergate and in answer to the committee's subpoena. The President's public speaking did not end here, however. On May 3 he appeared at a rally in Phoenix; on May 4 he spoke at Expo '74 in Spokane; and on May 11 he presented a commencement address at Oklahoma State University in Stillwater. All of these efforts were part of what has been referred to as Operation Candor, namely a program of carefully arranged appearances by the President in friendly territory—mainly in the South and West—in order to dramatize his continuing appeal.

But contrary to presidential strategy, the release of the transcripts and Operation Candor failed to stem the tide of criticism. Indeed, it surged anew when Senator James L. Buckley (Conservative-Republican, New York), whom many had criticized for urging the President's resignation on March 19, was joined by Republicans and Democrats alike in "suggesting" that it might be wise for the President to consider resigning rather than put the country through the agony of a presidential impeachment vote. The reason behind this deluge of resignation talk was that the conversations, now public, of the President and his assistants demonstrated what many felt to be a lack of moral principles on the part of those in the Oval Office. The earthiness of the President's language and his failure to put a stop to blatantly illegal acts seriously eroded his image and further weakened his failing credibility. By mid-May, even the staunchly conservative Chicago *Tribune* was calling for the President's resignation, and impeachment if necessary.

Meanwhile, Vice President Gerald R. Ford, replacing Spiro Agnew as the man nearest the presidency, had become, in effect, the working head of the Republican party. He campaigned for candidates in Illinois, Indiana, Kentucky, Michigan, New Jersey, Oklahoma, and Texas; gave commencement speeches at Eastern Illinois University, Texas A & M, and the University of Michigan; and replaced President Nixon as the man most Republicans wanted in their corner at election time. Not an eloquent speaker, he has been described as "wooden," with a "flat and earnest" voice. And wherever he went, he was asked his views on Watergate; generally, he supported the President while condemning those who were his primary aides. He attempted to "blend political appeals, accentuating the positive in the Administration, without dwelling on its Watergate problems" (Richard L. Madden, New York *Times,* February 15, 1974).

Like the Vice President, Cabinet members and other high officials were called upon to speak for the President and defend Administration policies. Secretary of the Treasury William E. Simon, in his former capacity as administrator of the Federal Energy Administration, made headlines with his pronouncements on fuel shortages; Interior Secretary Rogers B. Morton concerned himself with conservation problems; and Secretary of Agriculture Earl L. Butz dealt with food prices and shortages. Often facing hostile listeners, these and other public servants played their roles as best they could in an unpopular Administration beset by foreign, domestic, and ethical problems to a degree never before encountered.

James Reston observed that Washington had "settled down at least temporarily into a mood of frustration and disenchantment." According to the Gallup Poll, only 30 percent of those questioned approved of the way Congress handled its duties (only 25 percent approved of President Nixon); 47 percent disapproved; and 23 percent were undecided (New York *Times,* April 28, 1974). Evidence of "this weariness or disillusion" were "the inordinate number of resignations from Federal service." Nineteen Representatives (fifteen Republicans and four Democrats) and six Senators announced they would not seek reelection.

Many Senators, despite the pressures of congressional business and the concerns of the Watergate investigations, continued to accept outside speaking engagements. In fact, they reported $1,027,000 in earnings from lecturing for 1973, compared with $618,383 for 1972 and $787,438 for 1971. The latest available information (May 1974, since Senate rules require Senators to list their outside income from speeches and writing each May) shows that the most popular Senators speaking outside the Capitol before business, college, and political audiences were Democrat Hubert H. Humphrey of Minnesota, who earned $65,650, and Democrat James Abourezk of South Dakota, who reported an income of $49,425. Others who did very well on the speaking circuit include Barry Goldwater (Republican, Arizona), $44,733; Henry M. Jackson (Democrat, Washington), $39,575; William Proxmire (Democrat, Wisconsin), $38,625; Robert J. Dole (Republican, Kansas), $38,150; Thomas F. Eagleton (Democrat, Missouri), $36,950; Edmund S. Muskie (Democrat, Maine), $34,977; Howard H. Baker, Jr. (Republican, Tennessee), $34,350; James Buckley (Conservative-Republican, New York), $33,462; Mark O. Hatfield (Republican, Oregon), $33,250; George McGovern (Democrat, South Dakota), $28,700; Sam J. Ervin, Jr. (Democrat, North Carolina), $27,900; John G. Tower (Republican, Texas), $25,447; Vance Hartke (Democrat, Indiana), $24,750; John V. Tunney (Democrat, California), $22,518; Birch Bayh (Democrat, Indiana), $21,182; Harrison A. Williams, Jr. (Democrat, New Jersey), $20,295; Walter F. Mondale (Democrat, Minnesota), $19,426; Herman E. Talmadge (Democrat, Georgia), $19,135; and Harold E. Hughes (Democrat, Iowa), $19,450 (Rich Spencer and Miranda Lorraine, of the staff of the Washington *Post,* published in the Des Moines *Register,* May 20, 1974).

Lecturing continued to be a big business, perhaps grossing as much as $100 million annually, and in the words of Ralph Waldo Emerson, it provided "good bread" for its participants. Since the 1960s, Ralph Nader, Dick Gregory, Julian Bond, Vincent Price, Art Buchwald, and Alvin Toffler have been in great demand as speakers. One estimate suggests that Gregory, the social activist and former nightclub comic, earns close to $500,000 each year from his approximately three hundred visits to college campuses (James Lincoln Collier, "Live Lectures," New York *Times Magazine,* March 3, 1974). Other popular figures include Stewart Udall, Ramsey Clark, Shirley Chisholm, Rod Serling, and Gloria Steinem. The fee for a single speech usually runs from $500 to $3,000. For example, Associate Justice William O. Douglas received $3,000 for a lecture at the University of Texas (*National Observer,* March 16, 1974).

Even the principals in the Watergate scandal have been in great demand, with many invitations extended to Archibald Cox and Senators Howard Baker, Jr., and Sam Ervin, Jr. One enterprising agent even went so far as to book convicted Watergate burglar James McCord for a two-month speaking tour, at a stipend of nearly $80,000, but Judge John J. Sirica of the Federal District Court ordered McCord to cancel his plans.

At the time of this writing, Watergate is still with us and no one can foretell the future of President Nixon and his Administration. But the agony of Watergate will certainly continue for some time. Perhaps as a classic tragedy, catharsis will come within our private and public lives. As James Reston, always a perceptive observer of the American scene, recently wrote: "This process of renewal is going on in Washington these days underneath the headlines. Watergate was a virus, a disease in the body of the nation, and attention is now fixed properly on the agents of infection. But beyond all the arguments over the past, over impeachment and the definitions of impeachment, the corrective impulses of the nation are at work" (New York *Times,* March 22, 1974).

My sincere thanks go to many persons who have answered my queries, forwarded speeches, supplied background information, offered criticisms, and aided me in many other ways. As usual my colleagues in the Department of Speech at Louisiana State University have come to my assistance when I needed help. I am particularly indebted to Clinton Bradford, Stephen Cooper, Francine Merritt, Harold Mixon, Owen Peterson, Barbara Walsh, and my students. The project could not have been completed without the assistance of Linda Rewerts, Annette Sharp, Janet Fahey, and Holly McGowan.

WALDO W. BRADEN

Baton Rouge, Louisiana
July 1974

POSTSCRIPT

As this book went to press, the agonizing Watergate crisis was resolved by the resignation of President Nixon on August 9, 1974, and the succession to the presidency of Gerald R. Ford.

CONTENTS

VALUES, RIGHTS, AND LIBERTIES

THE POLITICAL QUESTION OF AMNESTY

THE VICE PRESIDENCY

THE AGONY OF WATERGATE

VULNERABILITY AND VIGILANCE [1]

ELLIOT L. RICHARDSON [2]

Watergate has resulted in suspicion and distrust of the Nixon Administration and has destroyed the political—and perhaps the personal—futures of many of Nixon's appointees and close associates. But the reverse has been the case for former Attorney General Elliot L. Richardson. After his refusal to submit to the President's demands to dismiss Special Prosecutor Archibald Cox (who subsequently was dismissed by Richardson's successor in what has come to be known as the Saturday Night Massacre), his popularity skyrocketed. To many Americans he is the epitome of the virtuous American man and has become, according to one source, "almost a folk hero" (Christopher Lydon, New York *Times,* January 13, 1974). In fact, almost immediately following his resignation as Attorney General, he began to be mentioned as a possible Republican presidential candidate in 1976.

Richardson, who had served with distinction as Secretary of Health, Education, and Welfare in the first Nixon Administration, in early 1973 was named Secretary of Defense. He remained there only three months, however, for when Attorney General Richard G. Kleindienst resigned on April 30, 1973, President Nixon named Richardson to replace him; the appointment was an attempt, most observers agree, to improve the tarnished image of his Administration. Because Richardson's confirmation by the Senate was made conditional upon his appointing an independent special prosecutor, Richardson brought back to Washington Archibald Cox, his old Harvard law professor.

Richardson has been kept busy since his resignation by filling speaking engagements and participating in Republican fund-raising activities in New Jersey, Ohio, Mississippi, California, and Texas. He has spoken at the Lyndon Johnson School of Politics at the University of Texas, the Chubb Fellowship at Yale University, and the Godkin lectureship at Harvard University. He reportedly already has speeches booked well into 1975.

[1] Delivered at the Appeal of Conscience Foundation dinner, Hotel Pierre, New York City, December 11, 1973. Quoted by permission.

[2] For biographical note, see Appendix.

As a speaker he has been described as "a reserved man, . . . handsome and immaculately tailored," who "comes across as being rather stiff in public appearances. Yet he offsets his serious demeanor with a wry, often self-deprecating wit" (Norman C. Miller, *Wall Street Journal,* February 22, 1974).

On December 11, 1973, Richardson spoke at the Appeal of Conscience Foundation dinner, at the Hotel Pierre, New York City. Honored on this occasion as "men of conscience" were Nelson A. Rockefeller, then governor of New York, and William J. Levitt, the builder. The dinner was attended by some five hundred diplomats, political figures, and religious leaders who support the Foundation's ecumenical efforts on behalf of religious freedom throughout the world.

Preceding Richardson to the lectern, Rockefeller gave a brief speech in which he said: "There is no denying that throughout the country there has been a blurring of the sharp focus on what is right and what is wrong. . . . Our present experience is making us realize that we as a people must return to our basic belief in individual honesty and integrity—whether in private or in public life. We must place moral principle above political advantage." The governor said that Richardson's "extraordinary intellect is matched by his integrity and devotion. Many young people will be influenced by his career that has got to be just starting."

The speech utilizes a problem-solution organization. The problem, of course, is his reactions to the Watergate investigations, or what he refers to as the "outrage at the prospect that an honest effort by the special prosecutor . . . has been aborted." Perhaps herein lies the value of the speech, for it gives a cogent statement by Richardson of his views on the tragic events that occurred during his tenure as Attorney General. The solution is a four-phase plan involving (1) protection against invasion of privacy; (2) prevention of campaign abuses; (3) erection of barriers against the improper use of political influence; and (4) stricter accountability in the exercise of power. This speech, like the one by Cox given elsewhere in this volume, is remarkable for its restraint. Richardson lived up to his reputation for being "coolly judicious."

Wise and learned men have been arguing for centuries about the status and sources of moral imperatives—whether absolute or relative, divinely inspired or socially conditioned, and so on. Centuries from now, God willing, wise and learned men will still be arguing about these same questions. Irrespective, however, of the basis on which moral imperatives rest, it seems clear that conscience is an instinctive response to their command. Either we obey our consciences or we suffer the almost physical discomfort inflicted by the failure to do so. Conscience is the voice of values long and deeply infused into bone and sinew and blood.

Conscience can, of course, have its narrow and self-righteous manifestations; it needs to be balanced by a sense of reality and, at times, by a sense of humor. There is a poem about New England by Edwin Arlington Robinson which contains the lines:

> Passion is here a soilure of the wits,
> We're told, and Love a cross for them to bear;
> Joy shivers in the corner where she knits
> And Conscience always has the rocking chair,
> Cheerful as when she tortured into fits
> The first cat that was ever killed by Care.

And Oliver Cromwell's entreaty to the Church of Scotland, although a useful reminder to all sorts and conditions of men, is apt to have special applicability to the man of conscience. "I beseech you, in the bowels of Christ," wrote Cromwell, "think it possible you may be mistaken."

The two distinguished men whom we honor here today are conspicuous for their own balanced and steadfast adherence to the dictates of conscience in situations of great responsibility and extraordinary stress. But what of people less responsible and less visible? A society has no collective conscience, after all, and the values of our own are rooted only as deeply as they are rooted in 200 million separate individuals. The evidence, in any case, on which to base a report on the State of the American Conscience is scanty and ambiguous, but not altogether lacking.

Take, for example, the public reaction to the Saturday Night Massacre. Three million messages descended upon the Congress, the greatest outpouring of its kind that had ever taken place. And for every person who took the trouble to write or send a telegram, there must have been many who felt like it, thought about it, but didn't get around to it. Though one of the "victims," I could not have guessed that all across the country were so many people who would feel so strongly about the day's events.

While it is still too soon to attempt any definitive interpretation of the public reaction to what happened, it's not too soon to make a stab at understanding it. It sprang in part, no doubt, from outrage at the prospect that an honest effort by the special prosecutor to get the truth had been aborted. It was a protest against what was widely perceived to be the breach of a commitment to his complete independence. There seems to have been an element, moreover, of hunger for a demonstration of willingness to draw a line on an issue of principle. As Oliver Wendell Holmes once remarked, "We live by symbols"; that Saturday's events provided the symbolic focus for a declaration of conscience on the part of the American people themselves.

But neither the fact nor the significance of this declaration of conscience can be understood except in terms of America's profound and conscientious concern with Watergate generally. To understand the response to the Saturday Night Massacre, it is necessary to understand why Watergate itself has had so powerful an impact.

At the time, the break-in of Democratic headquarters to plant a bug seemed remarkable chiefly for its clumsiness, and many were disposed to laugh the whole thing off as just another example of everyday political fun and games. That the "caper," as it was at first termed, could have been regarded as laughable is, in itself, a discouraging commentary on the low esteem in which the political process is held by all too many Americans. Not to be laughed off, however, was the cover-up of the break-in or the ensuing effluent of rancid revelations—from "dirty tricks" and the high-pressure inducement of illegal campaign contributions to abuse of intelligence-gathering techniques and institutions.

There were, to be sure, rationalizations: belief in the ends pursued—national security, domestic tranquillity, political victory; dedication to the cause; loyalty to superiors—all, within limits, laudable in themselves. But behind the layers of secrecy successively peeled back by persistent investigation we caught an ugly glimpse of the abuse of power. It has been a frightening glimpse, not so much for what it reveals as for what it portends. Like Ebenezer Scrooge appealing to the Ghost of Christmas Yet to Come, we find ourselves crying out, "Assure me that I yet may change these shadows you have shown me. . . ."

The subordination of means to ends is not new to American politics, of course, although more investigation and more research will be necessary to establish how much worse in degree have been the Watergate-associated perversions of power than those of past Administrations. The significant point, it seems to me, is this: Even if the evils of Watergate were assumed to be no worse than the kindred but unremarked acts of past Administrations, the fact that Americans now recoil from such things is a reassuring sign that our instinct of value-preservation is still alert and sensitive. Just as in a simpler age our forebears came to realize that they could no longer tolerate robber barons, we have come to realize that we can no longer tolerate the embezzlement of political trust.

Why has this happened? In law school I learned that most hard questions are questions of degree. I also learned that there can be a point at which a difference in degree becomes a difference in kind. Change taking place little by little, year by year, can by slow degrees bring about an accumulation which in the aggregate constitutes a fundamentally new situation. Meanwhile the old responses, the established adaptations to the earlier situation, have continued. Then, all at once, we become aware of the cumulative impact of the changes that have been taking place. We perceive, as if by a stroke of revelation, that the old adaptations and the old responses are no longer adequate.

So it has been with the steady coral-reef-like growth in the centralization, the pervasiveness, and the intrusiveness of governmental power. It used to be only the conservatives who cried "Wolf," and their cries were discounted because they often seemed to deny the seriousness of the problems perceived by others as demanding governmental solutions. But as expectations for the effectiveness of governmental action built up and the shortfall between promise and performance grew ever larger, a threshold was crossed, and many of us became convinced that the differences in degree had by now amounted to a difference in kind. Our society had reached a point where the necessity for choice and the need to make the process of choice more accessible and more responsive had converged in a greatly increased demand for simplification, decentralization, and citizen participation. This in turn gave new importance to the ingredient of honesty in government—to finding and facing facts, to learning what works and what doesn't work, to admitting that we don't know when we know we don't, to acknowledging failure and error—in short, to leveling with people.

All this was true before Watergate had acquired any more than a local identity as a fashionable address. But the most profound reason, I believe, why Watergate in all its new connotations has had so disturbing an impact is that actions which severally were not unprecedented have been the subject of an overflow of disclosures—themselves unprecedented—at a time when sensitivity to the pervasiveness and intrusiveness of government had reached that critical stage of degree I talked about a month ago.

For we are exposed as never before to the apparatus of government. Because government touches our lives in so many more ways than it once did—because we are so inescapably dependent upon governmental services and governmental protection—we are vulnerable as never before to the abuse of governmental power. Our awareness of vulnerability, moreover, is made all the more acute by the knowledge that technology has put into the hands of government an array of devices for monitoring, eavesdropping, and personal data processing whose potential for abuse must frighten anyone but a fool. In our new vulnerability we sense the need for a new vigilance.

These, then, as I see them, are the most basic factors accounting for the depth of public concern with Watergate and thus for the sharpness and scope of the reaction to the events of Saturday, October 20, which seemed for a time to signify the shutdown of any serious effort to pursue and punish the perpetrators of Watergate.

The investigation must go forward. The disclosures not yet made must be carried out fully and unequivocally. The gaps and omissions must be accounted for. But even when these steps are completed, the main task of restoring confidence will lie ahead. To accomplish this, a series of interrelated actions is required. These fall under four distinct headings.

The first is more secure protection against the invasion of privacy. The second is the prevention of campaign abuses. The third is the erection of barriers against the improper use of political influence. Fourth and finally is provision for stricter accountability in the exercise of power.

For each of these objectives concrete measures are both necessary and possible. This is not the occasion on which to describe them in detail, but each deserves brief mention.

In the case of the protection of privacy, one constructive step would be the issuance of clear guidelines for the use of all forms of electronic surveillance. Given existing constitutional constraints on intelligence-gathering for domestic purposes except by court order, this means in practice the adoption and publication of standards for the use of electronic surveillance for foreign intelligence-gathering. Another useful step would be to adopt the recommendations for the protection of individuals against the abuses of data-bank information systems which are contained in the recently published report of the HEW Advisory Committee on Automated Personal Data Systems. An important related measure would be enactment of the Criminal Information Systems Security and Privacy Act being developed by the Department of Justice when I left.

To curb campaign abuses, we can do something *now* about "dirty tricks" and dirty money. Because the former are not adequately covered by present Federal law, there is a need for a Federal Code of Fair Campaign Practices which would expressly prohibit such things as: belligerent or obscene phone calls falsely represented to be on behalf of a candidate, disruption of campaign operations or gatherings by paid political operatives, and transmission of sensitive political information by paid "political spies." As for excessive or under-the-table campaign contributions, the worst holes in the existing system could be plugged by a combination of ceilings on such easily monitored expenditures as those for television, radio, and newspaper advertising; a prohibition against cash contributions; and a limit on total contributions by any one person to a single candidate. Swift adoption of these safeguards would leave open for further deliberation and debate the exceedingly difficult issue of public subsidy of political campaigns.

With respect to the improper use of political influence, I would urge the extension to other departments and agencies of government of the kind of requirement I put into effect at Justice last August for the keeping of a record of contacts by outside individuals seeking to influence the disposition of particular matters. Without discouraging the legitimate communication of points of view that deserve to be heard, such a requirement would deter attempts to distort decision making by bringing to bear personal and political pressures unrelated to the merits. An expeditious way to accomplish this would be by executive order covering the entire executive branch.

Finally, as to accountability for the exercise of power, we the people have in our own hands the means of seeing to it that stricter standards are observed. Among the concrete, practical measures that we can insist be put into effect, some concern the more systematic exercise by the Congress of its oversight responsibilities. The Senate Judiciary Committee, for example, with my encouragement, recently established for the first time a subcommittee to oversee the activities of the FBI, and just two weeks ago former Solicitor General Griswold and I testified before a special committee cochaired by Senators Church and Mathias in support of legislation repealing emergency powers exercised in some cases since 1933 and creating regular procedures for congressional oversight of any emergency powers invoked in the future.

Within the executive branch, accountability can be reinforced by assuring greater visibility for the exercise of power. Where excessive secrecy prevents the public—individual citizens—from knowing what is going on, the barriers can be broken down by more consistent and more sympathetic administration of the Freedom of Information Act. This is the aim of a governmentwide study soon, I hope, to be launched under the leadership of the Department of Justice. And where responsibility has been blurred by excessive reliance on political amateurs who have not yet learned that it is not always smart to be smart, we can restore accountability by a return of authority to people who are both visible to the public and accessible to congressional interrogation. The result would be to strengthen the Cabinet in its advisory as well as its executive functions.

Untouched, however, by these limited measures are the risks of the abuse of central authority that arise from its uncontrolled growth over recent decades. Here the only worthwhile remedy is to reduce the scope of central authority itself while at the same time increasing the capacity of peripheral authorities to cope with the all-too-real problems we have been pushing toward Washington. It is harder, to be sure, to combine compassion and competence in fifty states and countless local governments and voluntary agencies than to let Washington do it. But the ugly glimpse of arrogance revealed by Watergate has given us an incentive that the abstract symmetry of the new federalism could never in itself have supplied.

The issue is no longer one simply of choosing the level of government best able to apply our resources and skills to the continuing reduction and ultimate eradication of poverty and ignorance or to the elimination of preventable crime and disease, although these goals must continue to claim our unremitting efforts. Rather, the transcendent issue of the foreseeable future will be to assure a place of dignity and respect for the individual person. We must rescue the individual from the homogenizing forces of a mass-communications, mass-production, urbanized society. We must restore his—and her—voice and stature and significance. We must recreate a sense of community and the mutual respect which springs from self-esteem.

In this renewal, conscience must be a goal as well as a guide. And its cultivation as a sure, instinctive response to what Judge Learned Hand called those "basic conflicts of 'right and wrong—between whose endless jar justice resides' " must be a first charge of all our teaching—that of the churches as well as the schools, that of parents as well as political leaders.

We are an honest people. We are a decent people. Our response to Watergate has proved that—both our disgust with what has been disclosed and our patience in awaiting proof of blame. Having surmounted Watergate—and we surely will surmount it—we shall have a new chance to achieve a higher, more widely accepted, and more deeply rooted consensus of political morality. It will be a brash and stupid politician indeed who does not heed this consensus. And we as a people will deserve our fate if we have not learned that as government grows bigger and more pervasive, the price of liberty is not simply vigilance but more vigilance.

Among my most treasured possessions is a photograph

of Judge Learned Hand on which the judge inscribed in Greek a passage from the *Iliad.* Archibald Cox had also clerked for Judge Hand, and during a phone conversation with Mr. Cox just before he was fired, I quoted this passage to him. It has special significance for this occasion. Literally translated, the passage reads:

"Now, though numberless fates of death beset us which no mortal can escape or avoid, let us go forward together, and either we shall give honor to one another, or another to us."

Let us go forward together.

PRESS CONFERENCE [3]

RICHARD M. NIXON [4]

The White House press corps gives constant and thorough coverage to the activities of the President, his family, and his staff. Whenever he wishes, the President preempts prime time on the three TV networks to give an address or make an announcement. In addition, he may grant an exclusive interview to a Barbara Walters or a Dan Rather, appear at a baseball game, dedicate a bridge or a park, or make a telephone call to an astronaut in full view of the cameras. He may open the White House to the media to report on a formal dinner, a wedding, the signing of an important bill, or the greeting of a foreign dignitary. Columnist Russell Baker has observed that "the President . . . is always news, whether he is involved in any news or not." Baker describes such presidential activity as a "pseudo event; that is, an event created to satisfy the media's ceaseless craving for something–anything–to be reported" (New York *Times Magazine,* April 17, 1974).

A press conference is another device used to bring the President and the media together. Franklin D. Roosevelt held 998 press conferences during his more than twelve years in the White House; Harry S. Truman, in seven years, formally faced the press 324 times; Dwight D. Eisenhower faced them 193 times in eight years; John F. Kennedy, 64 times in three years; and Lyndon B. Johnson, 126 times in six years. President Nixon, who has utilized the media far more often than any of his predecessors, has been reluctant to talk openly and on the record with reporters. In six years he has held only 38 news conferences.

Many believe that the President, because of his command of the nation's attention, has upset the balance between himself and his critics and thus, in the words of Fred W. Friendly (former president of CBS News), has managed to convert the media "into an electronic throne" (see Newton N. Minow and others, *Presidential Television,* Basic Books, 1974). The open press conference restores this balance, for it gives reporters the opportunity to

[3] Conducted in the East Room of the White House, Washington, D.C., March 6, 1974.

[4] For biographical note, see Appendix.

ask penetrating questions covering all facets of the nation's concerns and it exposes the President to full public scrutiny.

In late February and March, the President, troubled by the incessant "badgering" of reporters, finally succumbed to their wishes and began to hold press conferences. He held four of them: two at the White House, one before the Executive Club in Chicago, and one before the National Association of Broadcasters in Houston.

The press conference reproduced in this volume took place on March 6, 1974, in the East Room of the White House. After he made his opening statement, the President fielded nineteen questions from reporters, sixteen of them directed at various aspects of the Watergate affair. (For the sake of brevity, the three other questions and answers have been omitted.)

The President, not appearing to use notes, stood alone in the front of the room and turned from side to side to designate the questioner he wished to recognize. He maintained his composure throughout the session, and the reporters, too, were far more restrained than they had been on similar occasions. But they continued to press hard for clarification of Watergate issues —the President's memories of his crucial conference of March 21, 1973, and his reactions to the threat of impeachment. Although decorum was maintained and competition to gain the floor was less evident than usual, the atmosphere suggested tension and antagonism between the reporters and the President.

The confrontation seemed to conform to Roscoe Drummond's observation:

> Today the press conference is like a massive, three-ring circus with all the actors jamming one ring and nobody in charge. Dozens are on their feet screaming to be heard, and under President Nixon the atmosphere is charged with hostility. I cannot escape the conclusion that the whole thing is a disservice to the public, a liability to the press, and almost valueless to the President (*Christian Science Monitor,* January 9, 1974).

THE PRESIDENT: Won't you be seated, please.

Ladies and gentlemen, I have two brief announcements before going to your questions.

First, I want to congratulate on radio and television, Miss Helen Thomas for being selected as the White House bureau chief for UPI. As I understand it, Miss Thomas, this is the first time in history that a woman has been selected for that high post. We congratulate you.

Second, I also want to congratulate the members of the Senate who voted to sustain the veto of the energy bill. We are not necessarily associating you with that, Miss Thomas. [Laughter]

In voting to sustain the President's veto, the members of the Senate vetoed longer gas lines and vetoed nationwide rationing.

What we must now do is to move forward on the various measures that I have proposed that will accomplish the goal that this bill mistakenly was aimed to accomplish, and that is to get down the price of gasoline. That can only be done by increasing the supplies of gasoline and other types of energy.

That is why I trust that the Congress will move expeditiously on the proposals that I have made for the deregulation of natural gas, for doing something with regard to those measures in the field in the environment which restrict the production of coal, which could greatly alleviate the energy crisis, to the extent it is still a crisis; to go forward also on the Elk Hills production and exploration for oil in that Federal area and in the longer sense, to go forward with the various proposals that we have made for organization in the energy field, which will allow us to develop our nuclear power, new sources of energy and to achieve the goal we all want to achieve of independence for the United States for energy by at least and preferably before the year 1980.

I believe the way to get the price of gasoline down is to produce more and these measures which the Congress has had before it for a number of months should be acted upon in order to accomplish that goal.

Mr. Cormier, since Miss Thomas has already been mentioned, you get the first question.

QUESTION: Mr. President, your lawyer announced today that you will turn over to the House Judiciary Committee all of the materials that you made available to the special prosecutor. I am wondering, sir, what about other materials that the committee might want to see that the prosecutor didn't see?

THE PRESIDENT: Mr. Cormier, that matter has been under discussion, as you probably know, between Mr. St. Clair, White House counsel, and Mr. Doar, the counsel for the committee, and Mr. St. Clair has made, I think, a very forthcoming offer. He has indicated that we will respond to any written interrogatories under oath that the committee may have on matters that they do not think are covered adequately by the materials that have been submitted to Mr. Jaworski, and in addition, he has indicated that in the event that that is not satisfactory in order to bring the matter to a complete and, we hope, early conclusion, that the President will be glad to meet with members of the committee, perhaps the chairman, and the ranking minority member of the committee, at the White House to answer any further questions under oath that they may have.

As far as other materials are concerned, those matters will continue to be under discussion between White House counsel and Mr. Doar. It is the goal for all of us, I think, the goal of the committee—I think it would be theirs, it certainly is mine—to get a prompt conclusion to this matter as soon as possible.

And I would say further, that as far as the materials we have turned over, they include not only the famous subpoenaed tapes, which were turned over to Mr. Jaworski, but they include in addition to that, eleven additional tapes, a total of nineteen tapes, over seven hundred documents and enough material that Mr. Jaworski was able to say that he knew all and that the grand jury had all the information that it needed in order to bring to a conclusion its Watergate investigation.

Miss Thomas.

QUESTION: Mr. President, Mr. Haldeman, your former top aide in the White House, has been charged with perjury because he testified that you said it would be wrong to pay hush money to silence the Watergate defendants, and last August, you said that was accurate. Can you, and will you, provide proof that you did indeed say it would be wrong?

THE PRESIDENT: Miss Thomas, it would be improper, as, of course you know, for me to comment on the substance of any charges or indictment that have been made against any of the defendants in this matter. However, it is proper for me to comment on what I said and what I did on the twenty-first of March, which is the date in question.

On that occasion, Mr. Dean asked to see me, and when he came into the office, soon after his arrival he said that he wanted to tell me some things that he had not told me about the Watergate matter. And for the first time on March 21, he told me that payments had been made to defendants for the purpose of keeping them quiet, not simply for their defense.

If it had been simply for their defense, that would have been proper, I understand. But if it was for the purpose of keeping them quiet—you describe it as hush money—that, of course, would have been an obstruction of justice.

I examined him at great length. We examined all of the options at great length during our discussion, and we considered them on a tentative basis—every option as to what the defendants would do, as to who in the White House might be involved and other information that up to that time had not been disclosed to me by Mr. Dean.

Then we came to what I considered to be the bottom line. I pointed out that raising the money, paying the money, was something that could be done, but I pointed out that that was linked to clemency, that no individual is simply going to stay in jail because people are taking care of his family or his counsel, as the case might be, and that unless a promise of clemency was made that the objective of so-called hush money would not be achieved.

I am paraphrasing what was a relatively long conversation.

I then said that to pay clemency was wrong. In fact, I

think I can quote it directly. I said, "It is wrong; that is for sure." Mr. Haldeman was present when I said that, and Mr. Dean was present. Both agreed with my conclusion.

Now, when individuals read the entire transcript of the twenty-first meeting or hear the entire tape where we discussed all of these options, they may reach different interpretations, but I know what I meant, and I know also what I did.

I meant that the whole transaction was wrong, the transaction for the purpose of keeping this whole matter covered up. That was why I directed that Mr. Haldeman, Mr. Ehrlichman and Mr. Dean and Mr. Mitchell, who was then in New York, meet in Washington that evening, if possible —it turned out that they could not meet until the next day—so that we could find what would be the best way to get the whole story out.

I also know what I said with regard to clemency and with regard to the payment of money. I never at any time authorized clemency for any of the defendants. I never at any time authorized the payment of money to any of the defendants, and after we had met on the twenty-second, I sent Mr. Dean to Camp David to write a full report of everything that he knew.

That report was not forthcoming, and consequently, on the thirtieth of . . . [March] a week later, I directed Mr. Ehrlichman to conduct an independent investigation, which he did conduct, and presented to me on the fourteenth of April.

And also on the thirtieth, on that same day, Mr. Ziegler announced this to the press corps, after I had issued the direction, I directed that all members of the White House staff who were called by the grand jury should appear before the grand jury and testify fully with regard to any knowledge whatever they had with regard to their involvement if they were involved or anybody else's involvement.

In other words, the policy was one of full disclosure,

and that was the decision that was made at the conclusion of the meeting.

QUESTION: Mr. President.

THE PRESIDENT: Mr. Theis.

QUESTION: Without regard to past events or hush money or anything like that, would you now consider granting clemency to any former assistants who might ultimately be convicted?

THE PRESIDENT: The matter of clemency, Mr. Theis, is something that can only be granted and only be considered on an individual basis, depending upon the circumstances involved.

I can only say that under no circumstances has any defendant or potential defendant been offered clemency and none will be offered clemency. That would be improper and I will not engage in that activity. . . .

QUESTION: Mr. President, I would like to ask two questions, if I may. One is that you surprised a lot of us by calling a second news conference within eight days and I am wondering if that is the start of a new policy. And secondly, I would like to ask this question: It has always been the custom that foreign money from foreign citizens is permitted to be accepted and spent in American political campaigns at all levels and in your campaign in 1972, I think at least $150,000 came in from foreign citizens. Do you think that is right, and if not, will your campaign financing reform bill include a prohibition of that kind of money?

THE PRESIDENT: As a matter of fact, I think Mr. Harlow on, shall we say a leak basis, has already indicated some of the answers to the second part of the question.

The leaks in this case are correct. All contributions from foreign sources are prohibited under the campaign reform that we have recommended.

And going further, I think that you might be interested to know some of the other items that are actually going to be in the reform package. One is that all cash contributions are prohibited if they are above $50. All contributions in cases of presidential campaigns will be limited to $15,000 per person per candidate—in the case of congressional and senatorial campaigns, $3,000.

One of the points that we have ruled out—and incidentally, I am not touching on some unfair campaign practices and other items that are very interesting in the proposal because I want you to be able to write something Friday as well as today on this matter.

But I would say that among the other matters that I think are of particular interest to all of the members of the press is the fact that we believe that candidates should have a right to defend themselves against false charges that are made during a campaign, whether by their opponents or by the press.

Now, that is a very, shall we say, difficult ground in terms of the First Amendment and we will try to be very consistent with whatever the constitutional requirements are, but that is a proposal that we have considered.

One thing that we do not do, however, is to endorse public financing. I know there is a great deal of support for public financing in the Congress and it may be that eventually, if a bill does reach my desk, it will be in it.

I oppose it for this reason: The public financing proposals before the Congress, for the most part, are ones that would have the campaigns financed out of the general treasury. Now, what this would mean, very simply, would be that a taxpayer would be taxed to support a candidate or a party to whom he was opposed. That is not right. I think that that would, in effect, be taxation without representation.

So, therefore, for that and other reasons, I oppose public financing.

One of the other reasons, incidentally, is that I believe it is a healthy thing for people to contribute to campaigns and particularly in the smaller contribution areas.

I looked up figures, I found that 700,000 people contributed $100 or less to Senator McGovern's campaign. Over 900,000 people contributed $100 or less to the presidential campaign of our side. I think that kind of participation by people who in that way participate in politics should not be discouraged. It should be encouraged. In other words, I think campaigns should be financed by the candidates and not by the taxpayers.

QUESTION: Mr. President, to follow up an earlier answer, as I understand it, you said that you are not ruling out the possibility that you might grant clemency to a former aide. Is that correct, you are really not ruling that out, and if so, why?

THE PRESIDENT: No, Mr. Schram, I am simply saying that I am not ruling out granting clemency to any individual depending upon a personal tragedy or something of that sort.

What I am saying, that I am not going to grant clemency because they happen to be involved in Watergate. That I am ruling out.

QUESTION: Mr. President.

THE PRESIDENT: You had one last week, Clark, now. Mr. Healy.

In fact you had two.

QUESTION: Mr. President, many people are saying that Watergate played a prominent role in the election of a Democrat in the congressional district in Cincinnati yesterday. What is your opinion of that?

THE PRESIDENT: It might have. In fact, it was said also it may have had an effect on the election in Michigan.

But reflecting for a moment on off-year elections, and I know you are somewhat of an expert on this—of course, all of you are experts on off-year elections—a first point is that we have had six since the 1972 elections. The Republicans have won three, and we have lost three. In fact, yesterday we won in California, as you know, and when one Republican can beat eight Democrats in one race, that is a pretty good showing.

The other point is that as far as off-year elections, as distinguished from the British system where they seem to point as to what will happen in the general election, they seem to have exactly the reverse effect in this country.

For example, I found between 1964 and 1966 the Republicans won five, and the Democrats won seven congressional seats, and yet the Republicans won forty-seven seats in 1966.

Also, reflecting to the past, after General Eisenhower's landslide victory in 1956, we lost forty-seven seats in the House just two years later in 1958 because of a recession, and after President Johnson's landslide victory in 1964, his party lost forty-seven seats in the House, just two years later, because of a war.

This year we are not going to have a war, we are going to be making further progress toward peace—at least that is our goal and I think we will achieve it—and we are not going to have a recession.

So I believe that the dire predictions that are made as to what is going to happen in November because of what has been happening this spring will be proved to be wrong.

QUESTION: Mr. President.

THE PRESIDENT: Mr. Kempster.

QUESTION: Mr. President, in your answer to Mr. Cormier's question, you spoke of expeditious conclusion of the impeachment hearings in the House. Would it not serve the purpose of a speedy conclusion of these hearings for you to give the committee whatever materials, tapes and documents they consider pertinent to their investigation?

THE PRESIDENT: It would not lead to a speedy conclusion, it would delay it in my opinion, because if all that is really involved in this instance is to cart everything that is in the White House down to a committee, and to have them paw through it on a fishing expedition, it will take them not a matter of months so that they can complete their investigation, and we trust their decision by the first of May, which I understand is Mr. Rodino's object, but it would take them months and perhaps even as long as a year.

We will furnish the information we furnished Mr. Jaworski, the special prosecutor, all of which he considered to be relevant. We will furnish, as I have indicated, written interrogatories on any other relevant material, and we will also agree to meet with the chairman, the ranking member, as designated by the committee, to answer any other questions they may have. I believe that that will serve the purpose.

QUESTION: Mr. President, your attorneys have taken what is seen as the narrow view on impeachment, saying impeachment should be limited to very serious crimes committed in one's official capacity.

My question is, would you consider the crimes returned in the indictments last week, those of perjury, obstruction of justice and conspiracy to be impeachable crimes if they did apply to you?

THE PRESIDENT: Well, I have also quit beating my wife. [Laughter]

Of course, the crime of perjury is a serious crime and, of course, the crime of obstruction of justice is a serious crime, and would be an impeachable offense, and I do not expect that the House committee will find that the President is guilty of any of these crimes to which you have referred.

When you refer to a narrow view of what is an impeachable crime, I would say that might leave in the mind of some of our viewers and listeners, a connotation which would be inaccurate. It is the constitutional view. The Constitution is very precise. Even Senator Ervin agrees that that view is the right one, and if Senator Ervin agrees, it must be the right one.

QUESTION: Mr. President, Attorney General Saxbe has expressed the opinion that at some point in the impeachment procedure you might have to start paying for your own legal defense. Do you have any plans to hire your own lawyers, at your own, rather than at public expense?

THE PRESIDENT: If the Attorney General should rule that I should pay for my own defense, I shall, of course, do so.

I should point out, however, that I am not a defendant until the House passes a bill of impeachment. I would then be a defendant, and if the Attorney General of the United States should rule that the President should pay for his defense, I will find somebody to loan me the money. [Laughter]

QUESTION: Mr. President, I would like to follow up on a comment you made just a minute ago, where taking you back to March you said that you had ruled out immunity from prosecution of all your aides and in the same answer you said you wanted full disclosures of all of the facts about Watergate.

One of the purposes of granting immunity from prosecution is to get disclosures from a person who knows what is going on to crack the case. Some people have suggested that the order against immunity from prosecution was aimed at deterring John Dean from testifying and disclosing the facts.

How would you answer that thesis?

THE PRESIDENT: Well, on the contrary, I think that the use of immunity for any major White House employee would be highly improper. After all, someone who has the position of counsel to the President should come forward and testify as to everything that he knows and he should not require as the price for telling the truth getting immunity. That was my view then and it is my view now.

I should also point out that in the case of Mr. Ehrlichman and Mr. Haldeman and Mr. Colson, all of whom have been indicted, it is significant to note that none of them have used the shield of the Fifth Amendment as they could have and plead self-incrimination.

None of them have bargained for pleas, as they could have in order to get a lighter sentence. Each of them has testified freely before the committee, each of them has testified before the grand jury, each apparently believes in his innocence.

Under these circumstances, while they have been convicted in the press over and over again, while they have been convicted before committees over and over again, they are now before a court, and they are entitled to and they will receive from me, and I think from every fair-minded American, the presumption of innocence that any individual is entitled to because a court of law is the proper place for such matters to be decided. . . .

QUESTION: Mr. President, you said earlier, if my notes are correct, that on March 21, Mr. Dean told you for the first time that payments were made to defendants to keep them quiet and that you considered a number of options.

Did you not consider the option of blowing the whistle, of turning that information over to the authorities immediately, and on reflection now do you think that you should have?

THE PRESIDENT: As a matter of fact, among the options we considered was getting out a full report, a report that he would write. Among the options we considered the next day and we started to consider that day was to have everybody testify before the Ervin committee and waive executive privilege, which was a course of action which Attorney General Mitchell recommended.

Yes, the option of a full disclosure at that time by everybody concerned was one that was considered. The difficulty that I had was that for months these matters had not been brought to my attention. I had not been informed of the payments to the defendants. I had not been informed with regard to the alleged cover-up. I had not been informed about the possible involvement of some White House aides.

I felt it was my responsibility to conduct my own investigation with all of the assistance I could get from those who could provide information before moving to what would be a proper way of getting this story out to the country.

At all times it had been my goal to have a complete disclosure of this whole situation because, as you know, I have said there can be no cloud over the White House. I want that cloud removed. That is one of the reasons we have cooperated as we have with the special prosecutor. We will also cooperate with the Rodino committee. The facts will come out.

QUESTION: Mr. President, I have a follow-up on that question right there, on the March twenty-first meeting.

You have referred to your own personal desire to have complete disclosure and you have also mentioned here this evening that anybody who heard the tape of that March twenty-first meeting, or different people hearing that tape, or reading the transcript might get different impressions.

Have you ever considered the option of making that tape and transcript public so that the American people can read it and hear it and make their own judgment on what happened at that meeting?

THE PRESIDENT: Yes, I have. We have a problem there, however, in that that tape, as well as others, as was, I think, probably implied at least in the hearing today, affects the rights of the defendants and also the possibilities of the prosecution, and under the circumstances, of course, we must be, to a certain extent, guided by that.

I think eventually the entire tape will be made available, and as far as I am concerned, when any individual who is looking at it objectively, not only hears it or reads what the transcript is, but also sees what was done after that particular conversation took place, will conclude, first, that the President had no knowledge before the twenty-first, which Mr. Dean himself said when he came into the meeting; second, that the President never authorized clemency, in fact, rejected it on several occasions in that meeting; and third, that the President never authorized the payment of money to the defendants for the purpose of hushing them up.

QUESTION: Mr. President, you have spoken tonight of your willingness to take questions under oath in the White House from the senior Democratic and Republican members of the House Judiciary Committee. Would you consider, as an aid to rebuilding public confidence in your leadership and in speeding up the procedure, in taking questions in a public forum from the entire House Judiciary Committee?

THE PRESIDENT: This is a matter which I am leaving to Mr. St. Clair and Mr. Doar to work out as to what proper procedure could be developed. What I want is one that will get the facts, get them quickly, and one that will not delay the proceedings, but Mr. Doar and Mr. St. Clair are discussing the matter and I will defer any response until they have completed their discussions.

QUESTION: Mr. President, is Mr. Wilson, the attorney for Messrs. Haldeman and Ehrlichman, working with the White House or with you in concert in any way, and secondly, you have said that when others hear the tape of the twenty-first, they may well reach a different interpretation than the one you have presented tonight. Why is that?

THE PRESIDENT: Well, first, Mr. Wilson, of course, is not working with the White House, and neither are the attorneys for any of the other defendants. His only contact with the White House is one that would be perfectly proper in terms of information that a defendant or potential defendant would be entitled to.

As far as interpretations of tapes, not only this one, but others are concerned, any individual who wants to can take anyone's statement and interpret it any way he wants.

What I say is that I know what I said, I know what I meant, I know what I did, and I think that any fair-minded person will reach the same conclusion that I have repeated here several times tonight.

QUESTION: Mr. President, just to follow up an earlier

question about Watergate and the indictments, I was wondering if you figured out, sir, why the payment of $75,000 in alleged hush money occurred the same day you said you disapproved of the practice? I am talking about the March twenty-first conversation.

THE PRESIDENT: I have no information as to when a payment was made, to what you have referred. All I have information on is as to my own actions and my own directions, and my actions and directions were clear and very precise. I did not authorize payments and I did not have knowledge of payments to which you have referred. . . .

QUESTION: Mr. President, can I ask you—

THE PRESIDENT: Mr. Lisagor isn't with a wire service, but he always has a question.

QUESTION: —some legal scholars, including Senator Ervin, have said that the truth will never be fully established unless all witnesses subject themselves, or submit to cross-examination. Are there circumstances under which you would submit to cross-examination if it would serve to clear up this Watergate affair?

THE PRESIDENT: Well first, Mr. Lisagor, I will do nothing to weaken the office of the presidency. To submit to cross-examination under circumstances that would, in effect, put the President in the box when he was not indicted, in effect, by the House of Representatives—where he would be in the box if he went to the Senate—I think would be improper. However, as far as I am concerned, as I have indicated, I will have written interrogatories and I will be willing to meet with the ranking members of the Judiciary Committee, both of whom I understand are very good lawyers and very good cross-examiners, to take any questions that they may have if they have any at the conclusion of their own investigation.

THE PRESS: Thank you, Mr. President.

THE WATERGATE INVESTIGATION [5]

LOWELL P. WEICKER, JR.[6]

On December 2, 1973, from 6:00 to 7:00 P.M. EST, the Columbia Broadcasting System Television Network broadcast a debate on the proposition, Resolved: the Watergate investigation has been vindicated. This news special had been edited from a two-hour debate held on November 26, 1973, before the Yale Political Union at Law Auditorium, Yale University, New Haven. With two student colleagues (Deborah Rhode and Fred Krupp) Senator Lowell Weicker, Jr., of Connecticut presented the affirmative and William F. Buckley, Jr., and two student members of the Union (David Applegate and Ralph Cavanagh) defended the negative. The occasion was a homecoming for Weicker and Buckley, who are graduates of Yale and former members of the Union, and who had debated each other as students before the Union in 1950.

At Yale the four students gave opening speeches of two to three minutes, followed by constructive speeches by Weicker and Buckley. The debate was concluded by a brief rejoinder by Weicker.

Extracted from the debate for inclusion here is the main speech that Weicker delivered. It is reproduced as it was transcribed and reflects of course the Senator's oral style and his reactions to the immediate audience and occasion. The speech reveals how deeply he was moved by the Senate Watergate Committee's hearings and their implications. It presents an excellent summary of the case against the Nixon Administration.

Weicker, who is six feet six inches tall and weighs 250 pounds, is physically the largest man in the Senate. William V. Shannon concludes, "Morally and politically he grew to increased stature during the Watergate hearings. . . . Weicker's indignation at the chicanery and ruthlessness exposed in the hearings sometimes caused his words to come spluttering out slower than his mind

[5] Delivered before the Yale Political Union, Law Auditorium, Yale University, New Haven, Connecticut, November 26, 1973. Presented as a news special by the Columbia Broadcasting System, December 2, 1973. Quoted by permission of Lowell P. Weicker, Jr., and William F. Buckley, Jr., who owns the rights to the program.

[6] For biographical note, see Appendix.

and emotions moved. But the genuineness of his convictions came through clearly" (*They Could Not Trust the King,* Macmillan, 1974).

Mr. Speaker, and Bill, and opponents and partners, everybody at the Political Union, my friends at Yale:

Let me just respond, if I could, very briefly to two questions that were raised and—and one comment that was made in two speakers who preceded me.

First of all, as far as the question of resignation or impeachment: You can't have it both ways, as far as the element of fairness is concerned. My job and the job of the committee is not one of determining whether or not the President should be impeached; it's a question of fact-finding—and the job of impeachment, as you well know, belongs to the House of Representatives. And quite frankly, I would disqualify myself should impeachment ever come about and I had already called for the impeachment of the President of the United States or for his resignation. I would consider myself unfit to sit in judgment on that particular individual. This is the concept that was referred to by the first speaker—of fairness. It's the same attitude, I might add, that governs the committee and the committee's actions; to bend over in the area of fairness and to assure that we don't prejudge anybody or anything or—or any particular action.

Understand clearly that the job of the House of Representatives is very much like that of a grand jury. Theirs is the job of indictment. The trial concept comes into being before the United States Senate and, as I indicated to you, had I called at any point—up to now and including now—for the impeachment or the resignation of the President of the United States, then quite frankly I would consider myself disqualified to sit in—on his trial before the United States Senate if that should ever take place.

Point number two: [Applause] Times have changed as far as politics, as far as how you're going to go ahead and reform the system; you know, you just can't go ahead and wear an American flag in your lapel and—[Laughter] sit behind a bust of Abraham Lincoln and—and go ahead and —[Applause] have that suffice as being on the good side of all things. You gotta live America; the concept's too big to go ahead and reduce to a lapel pin or a bust of anybody. You gotta live it.

And as far as I'm concerned, I said from the outset—and I spoke as a partisan Republican in this sense—that the best politics was the best investigation. This democracy of ours is just becoming that—a real democracy where people out on the street can make just as good decisions as—as I can. What they want is the truth, and you're not going to go ahead and be able to give any slick answers or the usual political clichés to resolve this particular crisis.

I'm not through, naturally, with my job; that doesn't come to an end until February. But I can assure you, yes, I worry about the very point that the speaker made: Will the country go ahead and accept the facts that have been put before it or does it plan on living with a little bit of deceit and a little bit of decadence? And I'll get to that later on.

On May 17, 1973, the Senate Select Committee on Presidential Campaign Activities began its hearings, and this evening I'd like to highlight some of the important revelations of those hearings as they relate to American politics, to American Government, to our Constitution and our laws.

And my argument's not going to rely on speculation, or philosophy, or contested or refuted charges; only what is accepted fact.

Let's start off with politics. What you've seen isn't the politics of idealism. You've seen the politics of the gutter, only this time you can't say you didn't know about it; it's been put right out there on the table. And you and I and —and everybody in this country's got to go ahead and—and make a choice.

"Dirty tricks" now is no longer in the humorous category, but it consisted of the following: the Watergate break-in and the bugging—a formal attempt by one political entity (the Committee to Re-elect the President, not the Republican National Committee) to illegally gain information from the opposing party. This wasn't eight men gratuitously getting together in a barroom and deciding to go ahead and have some fun. This was well planned, well financed; spying on a formal paid basis. You heard that.

Disruption by stink bombs; disruption by sabotage of phone banks; and then you also heard on the other side the welcoming of violence—the welcoming of violence to the person of the President of the United States, in order to gain votes, by his closest adviser; and the uncontrolled uses of cash; the false telegrams; false advertisements; and the secret defense funds—yes, you know—left off in the phone booths, and the flower pots, and the trash cans, and the airport lockers.

And you heard about a man by the name of Ulasewicz, hired by the White House, by John Ehrlichman, paid in cash by the President's personal attorney to conduct secret investigations into the personal lives of politicians; what was desired was information to go ahead and use in the form of political blackmail.

And I remember at the time so many of the reporters in Washington saying, "You know, Senator, that's a pretty close one as to whether—you know—this is good or bad." And I came to realize then that, you know, maybe even Washington is sort of out of step with the rest of the United States. And it wasn't until a Harris Poll taken several months ago that the people of the United States—83 to 8 percent—came down on this particular type of activity.

But again—it's all right to refer to these things as "We're all against them and we're not here to defend them," but the fact is that these matters came to your attention and the attention of this country by the work of this particular committee.

And the arm-twisting of the corporations to make illegal contributions—you heard that only a couple of weeks ago.

Now let's move on to government, very briefly. Sitting in the Attorney General's office of the United States, you learned of the fact—the discussions of mugging, of bugging, of prostitution, kidnapping—all was a part of the plan to go ahead and find out what was going on inside the Democratic campaign. Not, mind you, in the office of the campaign director (I would disagree with that, also), but in the office of the man who was charged with the responsibility of protecting us all and of being the one person, if nobody else does, that's to uphold the laws of this nation.

And John Caulfield, who made the offer of executive clemency to McCord and McCord would take a dive and go to prison and keep quiet—John Caulfield, the special adviser to the President on law enforcement—this was his official capacity.

And Pat Gray, head of the Federal Bureau of Investigation. On June 28th he walks into a White House where—which he believed was the epitome of honesty and integrity. And he was given orders to go ahead and burn particular files. It's all right for all of us to look back at that particular case and say, "He should have known." But even to this day, people walk into the White House and they know a lot more than Pat Gray ever knew, and still they walk and still they're willing to get trapped in the mesh known as Watergate.

And his phone call to the President of the United States on July the sixth in which he warned the President—regardless of whether it's his version or the President's version, the warning was clear to our Chief Executive that something was wrong. And at the confirmation hearings when this man was up for the position of director of the FBI, you learned that even during the hearings one of the closest advisers to the President—Mr. Ehrlichman—made his famous statement of "let him hang and twist slowly," and you also heard the statement made by the President that "well, if Mr. Gray is that stupid, maybe he shouldn't be director of the FBI." And this was back in March, and then the President went ahead and learned of the burning of the files on April the fifteenth.

But there was no action taken to the director of the FBI because, after all, this was the institution that they wanted kept in place and wanted to have a leash on. And it wasn't until the period of April the twenty-fifth and twenty-sixth and twenty-seventh when Pat Gray called me to his office and all the facts were put out on the table, and finally he got out of the burning house, if you will. And the White House no longer had a hold on him and he had a chance to go ahead and—and tell the truth.

But the same information which he had told to me on April the twenty-fifth and twenty-sixth had been told to the President of the United States some two weeks earlier and no action had been taken.

And the use of the CIA to try and thwart the investigation; you've heard about that. And the facts of the press—not trying to earn the respect of a free press but rather to threaten the press via means of the IRS or the Justice Department or the FCC. These are now matters of record, matters of memoranda, not matters of speculation.

In conclusion, there are two points that I'd like to leave with you that hit into the area of the Constitution; we'll have more time to discuss these later.

First of all, the matter of the tapes: Remember this—were it not for this committee no one would have known the existence of taping machinery—recording machinery—in the White House. This wasn't brought out by any court or the free press; this was brought out by the committee. And it wasn't brought out, I might add, as really nothing has been brought out—by the White House, or by the President of the United States who's charged in my book and so far as our traditions are concerned with leading the quest for truth. Rather, it was brought out by the committee.

And I said at the time, during the hearings, that the

great problem that was going to arise here was not the constitutional confrontation between the executive and legislative branch of Government but rather between those individuals whose freedom would depend on the contents within those tapes or, on the other side of the coin, those whose guilt would be established by the content within those tapes.

And yet the tapes have been loaned to others. They've been given a special place in our justice system by the White House. And the confrontation has yet to be decided as to whether or not innocent men are going to go to jail because they're going to be denied the content—and some apparently will be denied that content—on the basis of what's happened to the tape, or whether or not guilty men will go free.

And Ellsberg: Probably nothing has gotten me as exercised as—as this particular series of events. It's not a question of whether you agree with Daniel Ellsberg or whether you don't agree with Daniel Ellsberg; the fact is I don't believe that any American should be convicted by illegal means, and this is exactly the situation that presented to itself—presented itself to the President when on March seventeenth—or the twenty-first, depending on which version you want to have—he was notified of the break-in in Dr. Fielding's office.

And on April 5th he had occasion to meet with the judge in that case during a session where they tried to get him to take the directorship of the FBI [laughter] and no comment was made as to this particular illegal action.

And on April—on the August twenty-second news conference by the President, he explained that the reason why he hadn't told the judge was that Henry Petersen had told him on April the eighteenth that this was a "dry well, a dry hole" that really had no relationship to the case. And then on April the twenty-sixth the President notified the judge of this information which he'd received on March seventeenth.

March the seventeenth to April the twenty-sixth. If nobody else in the whole United States will stand up on behalf of an innocent person or—assuring that a person will have his constitutional rights—do I expect the President of the United States? The answer is yes. And he didn't.

I started off on May the seventeenth, 1973, with a two-paragraph statement to the committee before its hearings started and I'm just going to repeat it now:

> Mr. Chairman and members of the committee: The gut question before this committee is not one of individual guilt or innocence. The gut question for the committee and country alike is and was how much truth do we want. A few men gambled that Americans wanted the quiet of efficiency rather than the turbulence of truth, and they were stopped a yard short of the goal by another few who believed in America as advertised.
>
> So the story to come has its significance—not in the acts of men breaking, entering and bugging the Watergate, but in acts of men who almost stole America.

And I say to you tonight that because of a free press and an independent judiciary, a select committee, they didn't, and more importantly, nobody will.

THE PRESIDENCY UNDER SIEGE

CREATIVITY IN LAW AND GOVERNMENT [1]

ARCHIBALD COX [2]

On Saturday, October 20, 1973, an event took place which has since come to be called the Saturday Night Massacre. That evening, both Attorney General Elliot L. Richardson and Deputy Attorney General William D. Ruckelshaus resigned from the Justice Department rather than comply with the wishes of President Nixon, who ordered them to dismiss Archibald Cox from his position as special Watergate prosecutor. Nixon then named Solicitor General Robert H. Bork acting Attorney General and it was he who dismissed Cox. Cox touched off the crisis when he refused to be a party to a deal which the President proposed concerning the Watergate tapes. Nixon offered to supply the grand jury and the Senate Watergate Committee with a summary of the tapes, to be verified by Democratic Senator John C. Stennis of Mississippi. When Cox defied the President and insisted upon direct access to the tapes, the chain of events leading to the "massacre" began.

The three departures were particularly dramatic because the President had originally appointed Richardson, already a Cabinet officer and a man of impeccable reputation, to the post of Attorney General to replace Richard Kleindienst, who had resigned April 30, 1973. Richardson, in an effort to reestablish confidence in a Justice Department tainted by disclosures of White House interference in its affairs, named Archibald Cox, his old Harvard law professor and former solicitor general, as special Watergate prosecutor. Known as "a troubleshooter with a passion for principle," Cox lived up to his reputation as a thorough and courageous man (Stewart Dill, *Christian Science Monitor*, May 22, 1973). Upon his dismissal, he was quoted as saying: "Whether ours shall continue to be a government of laws and not of men is now for Congress and ultimately the American people [to decide]."

The speech reproduced here is the one given by Cox at Am-

[1] Delivered as part of The Copeland Colloquium, Amherst College, Amherst, Massachusetts, January 22, 1974. Quoted by permission.

[2] For biographical note, see Appendix.

herst College, Amherst, Massachusetts, on January 22, 1974. His presentation was part of The Copeland Colloquium, the name given to a week of special events at the college that was highlighted by the visits of representatives from the arts—dance, theater, and music—and from fields not usually considered creative, but from which social innovation nevertheless arises—politics and public administration, science and the professions. The Cox speech was delivered in the Indoors Athletic Field before an estimated 3,500 persons, the largest indoor audience ever to attend such an event at Amherst.

Those who came to hear Cox speak were undoubtedly eager to hear what the ex-prosecutor would say about his recent experiences with the Nixon Administration. And he did not disappoint them, for by entitling his speech "Creativity in Law and Government," he provided himself with a large area of activity from which he could draw his material. Indeed, although he touched upon the matter of the creative contributions made by lawyers to public and private life, Cox devoted nearly half of his speech to the Watergate affair. He gave his listeners, in a tempered tone, his views on Watergate, impeachment, and the difficult problems facing the nation. He cast his speech on a high plane, and even when he mentioned his dismissal from office, he avoided seeming partisan. Rather, he suggested that the episode "can be made a turning point and therefore a blessing. It has shocked out of lethargy the conscience of the nation." The speech is a masterly presentation, showing careful construction and a meticulous choice of words. Instead of being emotional or moralistic, it is legalistic in tone.

At a time when World War II and the reconstruction of Europe were challenging the finest minds in the Western world Jean Paul Monnet, the great French economist and statesman, asked an American friend:

> Will you please explain to me why the men whom I regard as the most effective—the most fruitful, the most creative—are lawyers.

Not all agree. Sir Thomas More wrote that in Utopia

> They have no lawyers among them, for they consider [lawyers] as a sort of person whose profession it is to disguise matters, and to wrest the laws.

Utopia achieved there would indeed be no need for lawyers, nor for doctors—and perhaps not for butchers, bakers or candlestick makers. But until then lawyers are surely required, and I take enough pride in the best men of my profession to think that Jean Paul Monnet's observation upon the creativity of lawyers, stripped of invidious comparisons, was perceptive and correct. My plan this evening is to try to describe the creativity of lawyers, to carry the ideas over into government, and then to speculate about the sources of creativity in both areas but chiefly in government.

Of course the creativity of the lawyer is not that of the artist, the poet, the musician, or even the novelist, although one of the lawyer's tools, like the novelist's, is words. The challenging sphere of the men of law is formulating the rules and prescribing the procedures and forms of organization by which men and women may live and work together. Every practicing lawyer, whether he deals in constitutional issues, advice to corporations, collective labor agreements or wills and family relations is concerned with the concepts, the institutions, the rules and forms of organization that channel human endeavor. Lawyers are undoubtedly wordsmiths, for words are the tools for expressing intellectual concepts—concepts not emotions—with the degree of exactness and consistency necessary to rules by which persons can guide their activities in relation to each other and which, in appropriate cases, society can enforce.

I do not mean to leave the impression that the intellectual side of the law—the side that many students view as nit-picking and logic-chopping—is the whole story. The words and concepts the skilled lawyer finds so delightful as tools, must never become the master. The law's concern is men and women, their daily lives, their joys and sorrows, their fears and aspirations, their mean pursuits and high adventures. Without sympathetic understanding of life, perhaps without understanding the persons with whom he deals better than they understand themselves, a lawyer is not worthy of the name. But in the end he must work in intellectual terms, with reasoned analysis, concepts and words, because he deals chiefly in rules written either for private individuals seeking to order their future relations or by government in the form of law. Others understand human lives and activities as well as and often better than lawyers. The lawyer's uniquely professional contribution comes on the intellectual side in developing and articulating the forms of organization, procedures and other rules necessary to bring some degree of ordered cooperation, and therefore opportunity, to the affairs of men.

II

A few examples may illustrate my meaning.

The economic base of our society is mass production and transportation of goods and mass consumption. The development of both depended upon lawyers' ingenuity. Mass production and mass transportation depend upon the aggregation of the individual assets of many people, upon pooled and borrowed capital, and the pooling and borrowing require convenient rules covering the terms of the loan, the relations between borrowers and lenders or joint venturers, and the multitude of future contingencies. Today we know the necessary rules, institutions and concepts by the names of corporation, stock, bond, trust indenture, equipment trust certificate, etc. But these legal instruments did not exist two hundred years ago; some lawyer had to conceive them. Sometimes true imagination on a large scale was necessary, sometimes only a small refinement; but in either case the corporate and financial instruments are not the products of natural evolution like tigers, mice and men, but of human creativity. Take the conditional sales contract or its British version the hire-purchase agreement as an example. The arrangement is now as familiar as the wheel, and familiarity has made it as hard as it is in the case of the wheel to understand the true inventiveness required for the conception. But in the beginning the conditional sale was some lawyer's exceedingly bright idea and, despite many abuses requiring reform, it or something like it was and probably still is essential to the material base of our civilization.

For a second example consider industrial relations. Surely one of the great areas of human progress in the last half century has been in the lot of the industrial wage earner, through labor unions and collective bargaining. Through the unions' countervailing power real wages have been protected or increased, job insecurity has been minimized, and a large measure of industrial justice for individual workers has been brought into the mine, mill and factory. The basic needs were recognized without lawyers. No legal skill or training was required for the idea that workers should band together and require the employer to deal with them as a group. Lawyers did play major roles, although perhaps they were unnecessary, when it came time to give government protection to a right to form, join and assist labor unions, to put employers under a legal duty to bargain collectively, and to borrow the principle of majority rule from the political sphere. But these general ideas need both corollary rules to give them substance and procedures and institutions for carrying them out. Collective bargaining agreements had to be written to which individual workers would look as a source and definition of rights; grievance procedures and a system of arbitration had to be developed to administer the agreement in the case of disputes; and the industrial law of the plant had to be integrated with the courts and conventional legal system. In these areas constructive and imaginative lawyers were extraordinarily useful if not indispensable.

Turning from what the legal profession calls private law to government, we should probably all agree that the most creative acts in our political history were done at the Philadelphia Convention in 1787 and under Chief Justice Marshall during the first third of the nineteenth century. The Convention created a new and unique form of federal union in which both state and Federal governments deal directly with the same citizens in the same geographical area, each with its own taxes, courts and administrators, each assigned a functional jurisdiction sometimes overlapping the other's.

Apart from the steadying influence of Washington and Franklin, the leading figures at the Convention were all lawyers. I do not know whether they fully understood the complex federal system they originated or simply provided the seed idea which others rationalized and nurtured. Either way theirs was an extraordinarily creative legal and political idea, not only in the sense that it was markedly original but also in its generative power. John Marshall's notion of judicial review of both Federal and state legislation had legal antecedents, but it was a marked advance and provided another uniquely American institution of government which is enormously useful in protecting the individual against government and probably indispensable to the operation of the federal system.

III

For my final example I turn to the inquiry of the Judiciary Committee of the House of Representatives into the proposed impeachment of President Nixon, looking ahead to possible impeachment by the House and possible trial and conviction in the Senate. Here the lawyers particularly but also the men in government and other forms of public life, indeed all of us, face novel and unusually difficult challenges to our creativity. We write upon an almost-clean slate. Little law or political precedent is available to guide the hard decisions. Yet, regardless of the outcome, the value of the proceeding will depend upon whether the process is so conducted that the country perceives it as a fair and legitimate measure for restoring integrity to government. If President Nixon should be impeached and convicted, the question of legitimacy will be paramount. If President Nixon is acquitted, the country will still need assurance about the integrity of that conclusion. Whatever the event, we may fairly ask that the leadership build better for the future than their predecessors at the impeachment of Andrew Johnson.

The central challenge is to formulate the principles—the

general standards of conduct—by which a President is to be judged in a proceeding that vacates, without direct expression of the popular will, a choice made by the people—in this case overwhelmingly made by the people—in the regular election only a few years before. Too much discussion, both public and private, has been concerned either with loose generalities about the ultimate question of impeachment *vel non,* or with the excitement and speculation stirred by particular disclosures. Too little hard debate has focused upon what should be impeachable offenses—upon why some wrongdoing should be grounds for impeachment while other misconduct is left to popular judgment at the polls. I am convinced that the legitimacy of the final conclusion in the view of the American people will depend upon the success of counsel and other public men in formulating general standards of conduct fairly applicable to any President and in educating the public upon their meaning and legal and moral base. For Democratic Senators and Representatives to keep silent upon the ground that impeachment is a Republican problem and for Republicans to keep silent while they test the political winds is to deny the country the debate necessary to educated self-government and the development of governmental institutions.

A priori we might give any one of three polar meanings to the "high crimes and misdemeanours" for which a President, a judge or any other civil officer may be impeached.

(1) William Giles, President Jefferson's majority leader in the Senate, advised his colleagues during the proceedings against Supreme Court Justice Samuel Chase that "impeachment is nothing more than an enquiry, by the two houses of Congress, whether the office of any public man might not be better filled by another." Justice Chase was acquitted. The view of impeachment expressed by Giles never again had serious support (unless one counts as "serious" the speech of Congressman Gerald Ford a few years ago advocating the impeachment of Justice Douglas).

(2) The strictest view of the constitutional phrase "high crimes and misdemeanors" holds that impeachable offenses are confined to violations of the criminal law and to "high," i.e., very serious crimes, whether felonies or misdemeanors. This reading has better standing than the first, but the weight of the argument is against it.

The English parliamentary precedents, which were familiar to the Founding Fathers, included instances of noncriminal conduct and, although the Founding Fathers desired to cut back on the precedents, the constitutional phrasing makes it unlikely that they chose technical criminality as the line of demarcation. In the late eighteenth century "misdemeanor" was often used as a synonym for any misbehavior, rather than to describe a criminal offense not punishable as a felony. Since the Constitution speaks first of "crimes," giving "misdemeanors" its technical meaning in the criminal law renders it merely redundant, unless the aim is to authorize impeachment not only for "high crimes" but also for "petty misdemeanors," such as making excessive noise in a public place, racing an automobile or blasphemy. This seems unlikely. The recorded debates at the Philadelphia Convention and the subsequent expositions of the framers also make it pretty clear that impeachment was intended to be a vehicle for dealing with officials whose wrongs require removal from office even though not technically criminal. Refusal to perform the functions of an office while clinging to the status and perquisites seems a good illustration.

(3) We are left with a third view; i.e., that "high crimes and misdemeanors" covers some but surely not all "political," in the sense of governmental, offenses.

Reaching this conclusion moves us along, but it is only the beginning of the challenge. What are the wrongs against the people, the body politic, for which a President may properly be impeached?

It would be easier if history provided a list of legitimate grounds for impeachment, but the only precedents are scattered pretty far afield from current issues. Working with a clean slate, perhaps we can best begin by asking what deep-seated needs any rule we formulate must satisfy.

The Gallup Poll and like measures of public opinion report that a very large majority believe that President Nixon is guilty of covering up wrongdoing, but of those expressing an opinion, a majority oppose removal by impeachment. The difference, in my opinion, is attributable to a fear of impeachment not unlike the fear of regicide and the horror of the regicide once accomplished during the time of Cromwell and King Charles I. Of course, impeachment cannot be wholly illegitimate—the Constitution provides for it—but I think that the country has a deep, intuitive understanding that impeachment is extraordinary, radical surgery, legitimate only upon some equally fundamental wrong, doing such grave injury to the nation as to make any incumbent's further continuance in office unacceptable even though his previous entitlement was based upon popular election.

Surely any wrong so fundamental as to require setting aside the results of one election without holding another must be one that can be stated in general terms plainly applicable to any President at any time. The need is to quiet the fear that impeachment may be or become a partisan substitute for a premature election. Political opposition, emotion, dislike, distrust, and lack of public confidence (which may be temporary even when mixed with suspicion of some kind of wrongdoing) are not enough.

Equally surely, in my opinion, any general standard of political conduct the violation of which would support impeachment must have a broad and generally accepted moral base, understood by the country, so that again the same rule would apply to any President, so that we should not be resolving questions of public policy by impeachment nor should we be making up new rules of conduct as we go along.

Of course, it is unnecessary to draw up a complete code of presidential conduct. Mixing pragmatism with principle is one source of much of the creativity in Anglo-American law and government. We work eclectically up to a point, passing judgment upon particular sets of facts, but we also test our judgment by asking whether it rests upon reasons that we can articulate and apply to other situations having the same essential elements, with enough generality both in scope and continuity, to give guarantees against caprice, prejudice, self-interest or unreasoned emotion.

So here, the articulation of minimum acceptable standards of conduct for any President or high executive officer can begin with facts proved or assumed. It is fair to say that evidence may be available to show that President Nixon's lawyers and accountants, without deliberate misrepresentation, zealously sought every loophole and cut every corner in an effort to avoid or minimize the payment of taxes; to show that others acting on his behalf likewise stretched every possible point to add to the convenience and comfort of Key Biscayne and San Clemente at public expense; and, finally, to show that in some cases they claimed more than the law allows. Bad taste? Surely. Avaricious? Yes. Bad leadership? Again, surely. Morally shabby? I think so, even though the same shabbiness infects thousands of tax returns and expense accounts. Grounds for impeachment? I wonder. We are hardly prepared to say that any officer of the United States who, without concealing or misrepresenting material facts, claims a tax deduction not due should be removed from office. If not, does my phrasing omit some essential element in President Nixon's situation? What makes the omitted element decisive?

Let us try again. Is it tolerable or a high offense against the liberty and security of a whole people for a President to approve in principle electronic surveillance, mail covers and burglaries for the purpose of gathering domestic intelligence, over the objection of the established agencies to set in motion a small force of his own irregulars—the Caulfields,

Ulasewiczes, Liddys and Hunts—who will operate from the executive offices outside all the regularizing rules and procedures of the established agencies in order to effectuate Administration policy and political objectives, and to hamper inquiry into their activities?

Move to a third area. The President's duty is to see that the laws are faithfully executed. Is it an impeachable violation of this responsibility for him to refrain for months from any form of personal intervention when there is first suspicion and later at least some evidence that his highest personal aides and party officials are obstructing justice by covering up criminal misconduct, for him to withhold disclosure and refuse evidence when investigation leads to papers taken into his files, and for his aides, apparently with his approval, to cooperate with those seeking to avoid indictment and conviction?

I do not imply answers to these questions, nor do I suggest that my factual predicates represent the actual facts. The evidence may show more or less. The point I wish to emphasize is that it is past time for all those deeply concerned with our government to bend some of their time and effort away from the fun of factual disclosures to the very arduous task of formulating and thus creating a substantive law of impeachment where now there is none. Whether the present proceedings help to rebuild confidence in our system of government or push us further down the slope to cynicism and despair will depend upon the ability of the House Judiciary Committee to sense the as-yet-unstated moral intuition of the country and articulate it in operative principles by which President Nixon's conduct can be judged.

The task is one for the theorists and practitioners of political science as well as lawyers; it is also typical of the lawyer's creative art.

IV

Some may wonder whether I mean to portray the lawyer and even the government man as so heavily a technician and, if I do, whether the truly creative man is not the dreamer who perceives the broad ills of society, outlines the remedies, and inspires the mere technicians. I stress the intellectual nuts and bolts for several reasons:

(1) This is the most distinctive side of the law. Lawyers can dream as well as other men and sometimes better, but the reforming dreams are not confined to lawyers.

(2) The nuts and bolts, the nitty-gritty, is essential to the creation of meaningful new social, economic or political institutions. The artistic dreamer may see cathedrals in the clouds or in the flames of a hearth fire but he cannot build cathedrals without knowing the laws of mechanics, of stresses and strains and the capacities of stone and steel and bricks and mortar. For the Gothic cathedral one needed the spirit reaching towards God but also the flying buttress. The lawyer and government men are the architects of social, economic and political organization.

(3) Although others may be dreamers, the lawyer with great professional skill seems to be uniquely placed for creativity. Familiarity with the technical concepts, rules and institutions, public and private, that may order the affairs of men encourages new ideas not only because it gives an appreciation of the flow of invention but also because it carries the sense of power and capacity that is one of the sources of creativity in any field.

The last point is easily pressed too far. The lawyer too caught up in the present law is often an obstacle to change, and existing institutions, I think, are themselves impediments to new arrangements in both law and government. To illustrate, we shall always need a strong presidency but surely there is also need for new mechanisms securing greater responsiveness and responsibility to the people's other representatives and much freer flow of information. If we could sweep the chessmen off the board and start afresh, perhaps some form of parliamentary government would be preferable, but all the forces suggested by words like habit, tradition, expectations and continuity work so strongly against the acceptability of such a change as almost surely to prevent it. Those forces, even as we resist them, press for meeting the need by successive smaller, separately interstitial measures that may revolutionize even though each alone seems not too inconsistent with the basic structure. Similarly, the reform of the government of metropolitan areas would be vastly easier without the incubus of existing city, country and state boundaries. Not even a violent revolution can wholly wipe out the restrictions of the past. The expert in the existing rules has perhaps the best chance to perceive how they can be changed.

But when these things are said, I must confess that the law itself contains few of the ultimate forces generating creativity. The British legal philosopher, Lord Radcliffe observed:

> The law needs a compass to guide it. What drives us [lawyers] back from time to time to search further, to question outright what are our purposes is the insistence of the layman, the man who is not versed in law, that it shall stand for something more, for some vindication of a sense of right and wrong that is not merely provisional or just the product of historical forces.

I would answer that the law has one generative commitment—the goal of civility, the commitment to ordering the affairs of men with a minimum of force and maximum of reason and respect for human personality. The commitment is vastly important but, except for this, Lord Radcliffe is right. To return to my metaphor, the spirit that made Gothic cathedrals reach towards God, the forces that set the goals of a society, the ultimate sources of creativity lie outside the law and even government, even though they may infuse political leaders and the legal profession.

V

What can we say of those sources and therefore of the chance of renewed creativity in law and government? I can offer only a few random observations.

Surely one of the springs of creativity in the government of any free society is the spirit of cooperation that used to run deep in the American people. Alfred North Whitehead observed that no other people in the history of mankind had ever shown such innate qualities of toleration and cooperation. The will to cooperate flows chiefly, I think, from mutual trust and confidence in the importance of what I can only call the goals of the joint adventure in which we are all engaged. In a free society confidence in the goals of the enterprise is confidence in mankind—and ourselves.

Do these qualities survive in the realm of government? Confidence in the institutions of government and mutual trust between the elected governors and the governed had begun to erode long before Watergate, but surely the danger of a long slide into general cynicism, distrust and despair has been intensified by the evidence giving reason to believe that power, position and the very processes of government were criminally perverted at or near the very highest level of executive office for the sake of building or perpetuating personal and political power. The first essential in reversing the trend is restoration of confidence in the integrity of government.

The process will be slow and hard. Some steps are but the fair administration of justice: the continued vigorous investigation of the Watergate affair, the successful prosecution of offenders, the careful and impartial, but unrelenting, pursuit of the question of impeachment. Other steps must be legislative: for example the quick substitution of public financing for private contributions in political campaigns.

Still other steps can be only described as moral. Above all else we need to restore to government a stronger appreciation of the line separating fundamental judgments of right and wrong in the conduct of government and political life, on the one side, from mere political loyalties and political opinions on the other side. Too many of us grew up in an atmosphere of positivism and relativism in which the assertion of moral imperatives was taken as proof of ignorance and naiveté, at least among those wishing to be supposed persons of experience and sophistication. Others took the imperatives for granted, supposing that the fundamentals would look out for themselves. The cynics found justification in Leo Durocher's "Nice guys finish last," or in presidential aide Charles Colson's "It's only hard-nosed politics." One way or the other, success in gaining power took precedence and personal or party loyalty became a justification for silently going along if not actually participating in wrongdoing. It is time for a change.

The question remains whether, in a broader sense, we retain the innate spirit of cooperation of which Whitehead wrote and the belief in the goals of the enterprise on which I think it depends.

It is harder to have such confidence today because we have learned so much about ourselves. The quick conquest of a continent and the Horatio Alger story bred a folklore of endless resources and easy success. For all but the unfortunate, technology and industrial organization poured out a seemingly endless flow of material comforts. American might in two wars led us to suppose that our power extended to the farthest reaches of the globe. Recent decades dispelled these illusions. Our cities became unlivable. The succession of new cars, new television sets and new refrigerators proved a wasteland. Our power in the world is limited. We have lost our innocence and learned our capacity for evil; witness the bombs dropped on Southeast Asia and the gap that still exists between our pretenses and practices in the treatment of blacks, Chicanos and native Americans.

It takes honesty and courage to face these facts, but those whose realism leads them to despair suffer their own form of illusion. The men and women who sought freedom across the seas, who crossed the prairies and the great plains to conquer the mountains and build gardens in the desert, knew the costs, the struggle, the defeats and disappointments. They knew their fallibility and capacity for evil. But our forebears also had the greater insight for a vision of the ultimate perfectibility of man and the greater courage to pursue their vision even when they knew that neither they nor their children nor their children's children would wholly achieve it. Edward Everett Hale voiced the true spirit of those who pursued the American dream—

> I am only one,
> But still I am one.
> I cannot do everything,
> But I can do something . . .
> What I can do I ought to do . . .
> And what I ought to do by the grace of God I will do.

If you will forgive an even more personal thought, I add this final word!

Watergate can be made a turning point and therefore a blessing. It has shocked out of lethargy the conscience of the nation. Possibly my view is too self-centered and too much influenced by the moving letters I still receive, but it seems to me that the "fire storm"—to borrow a phrase from General Haig—which exploded over the weekend of October 21-22 had its source in the longing of countless simple, direct and moral people for a new measure of candor, simplicity and rectitude in the conduct of government—and for a confidence in them that would bespeak our confidence in ourselves. The turn of events was extraordinary. On a Friday and Saturday the President announced that he was discharging the special prosecutor, terminating independent investigation of the Watergate affair and related offenses, and refusing to produce relevant tapes and documents in accordance with the order of a court. The public outcry forced an immediate 180-degree turnabout. Within days, the court was assured that the tapes and documents would be produced. Within weeks, the independence of the Watergate special prosecution force was restored, the staff was retained unimpaired, and a vigorous and independent special prosecutor was appointed. This sequence of events demonstrates better than any other occurrence within memory the extent of this country's dedication to the principle that ours is a government of laws and not of men. It gave proof of the people's determination and ability to compel their highest officials to meet their obligations under the law as fully and faithfully as others. On this occasion, as so often in our history when fundamental questions were at stake, the people had a far better sense of the goals of the enterprise and needs of the nation than those claiming wider experience and greater sophistication.

The spirit is there. The power is there. The question is whether those who seek to be political leaders have the wit and will to evoke that spirit, articulate it, and take measures restoring confidence in the integrity of the government.

EITHER IMPEACH . . . OR GET OFF HIS BACK [3]

GEORGE D. AIKEN [4]

In the view of many Americans toward the end of 1973, the Watergate investigations had dragged on too long. Some members of Congress, they felt, were attempting to exploit the investigation for partisan advantage and others were timidly looking for a way to escape the embarrassment of pressing charges against the President. A growing number of citizens began to express greater concern for the office of the presidency than for Richard M. Nixon himself.

Addressing himself to that concern on November 7, 1973, the Republican dean of the Senate, George D. Aiken of Vermont, made one of his rare speeches. The essence of his message was a quotation from a constituent named Pete, who had written: "Either impeach him or get off his back!" Senator Aiken, known for his directness and honesty, pointedly said: "I don't want to contribute . . . to the destruction of the third presidency in a row."

The speech draws its power from its simplicity and the credibility of the eighty-one-year-old Senator, who has announced that he will not seek reelection. It was reported that the Vermonter received a favorable mail and telephone reaction to his speech (*Congressional Record,* November 20, 1973, S20880).

Ever since last March when the series of events, real and imagined, wrapped up in the word *Watergate* began to dominate our public life, I have issued no prepared statements on this subject.

I have not spoken out because, in company with millions of others, I haven't discovered an easy way of escaping our present predicament.

I don't want to contribute in any way to the destruction of the third presidency in a row.

[3] Delivered in the United States Senate, Washington, D.C., November 7, 1973. Quoted by permission.

[4] For biographical note, see Appendix.

At the same time, the White House has handled its domestic troubles with such relentless incompetence that those of us who would like to help have been like swimmers searching for a way out of the water only to run into one smooth and slippery rock after another.

Under our Constitution, the duties and responsibilities of each of the three branches of our Government are set forth.

Congress's tasks are to legislate and to hold the President and the executive branch accountable for administering the laws.

These are highly technical tasks, demanding above all else cool heads and a strict adherence to established procedures.

Submission to the politics of righteous indignation makes it impossible for Congress to do its job.

It tends to make us look foolish and incompetent.

I am speaking out now because the developing hue and cry for the President's resignation suggests to me a veritable epidemic of emotionalism.

It suggests that many prominent Americans, who ought to know better, find the task of holding the President accountable as just too difficult.

It suggests that the procedures laid down in the Constitution are just too complicated.

It suggests that most of the American people can't be trusted to keep their cool because some of them can't keep theirs.

Those who call for the President's resignation on the ground that he has lost their confidence risk poisoning the wells of politics for years to come.

Within less than ten years we have seen one presidency destroyed by an assassin's bullet; another by a bitter and divisive war.

To destroy the third in a row through the politics of righteous indignation cannot possibly restore confidence either at home or abroad.

It can only sow the seeds of suspicion and cynicism in our land and in our relations with other lands, inviting a harvest of whirlwinds such as mankind has never seen.

The men who wrote our Constitution were fully aware how waves of emotionalism, if given an easy electoral outlet, could reduce any political system to anarchy.

That's why in a nation governed by its laws they provided that Presidents should rule for four years.

They laid down that that period of rule could be interrupted only after Congress had framed a charge of high crimes and misdemeanors and had conducted a trial itself based on those charges.

To ask the President now to resign and thus relieve the Congress of its clear congressional duty amounts to a declaration of incompetence on the part of the Congress.

If I read correctly the signals sent out by the judicial branch of Government, they are also saying that Congress is the place where this crisis must be resolved.

The President hoped to get from the Supreme Court a "definitive" ruling on executive privilege, but the judicial system is telling us that much time and evidence must pass before any such ruling will be forthcoming.

That is how I read the decision of the Court of Appeals over the question of taped evidence.

That court clearly directed all parties to seek compromise before coming back.

It follows as night does day that the Supreme Court was and is not ready to accept this case now.

I wish Archibald Cox had enlightened us a little on this situation in his press conference.

He gave us a masterful lecture on the rules of evidence and on how, if he couldn't get the evidence he seeks, persons who had violated the law might not get a just punishment.

But above and beyond the punishment of individuals lies the question of the President's fitness to serve.

Only the Congress can judge that—the Congress and the voters at duly scheduled elections.

The desperate search for a special prosecutor, with the virtues of Caesar's wife and the unfettered authority of her husband, only represents another effort to escape responsibility.

It makes no sense to me to ask the President to prosecute himself, yet any special prosecutor in the Justice Department will find himself in that ridiculous position.

I was not at all surprised that Archibald Cox was fired; I was more surprised that such an intelligent and experienced man didn't quit first, or turn down the job in the first place.

Nor does it make sense to me for the Congress to ask the judicial branch to create a special prosecutor.

Aside from the fact that it will take a lot of time and litigation to establish the constitutionality of such an act, the result isn't likely to change matters one whit.

So long as the judicial branch does not want to render a "definitive" decision on executive privilege, ways will be found to avoid such a decision.

And the longer the process, the more obvious it will become that it is the Congress and only the Congress that has the duty to act.

Of course, if the President resigns, we will be relieved of our duty.

But I fail to see any great act of patriotism in such a drama.

On the contrary it is the President's duty to his country not to resign.

That which the American voter has done let no man undo except through due process.

That should be the President's guiding commandment.

It has been suggested that the President appear as a witness before the Senate Select Committee or, perhaps, some other.

This would appear to be another desperate search for a means of evading congressional responsibility.

The President's public explanations of the Watergate mess have been astonishingly inept.

But this is not of itself an impeachable offense nor does it suggest that the President be scolded, publicly, in the presence of a congressional committee.

If Harry Truman were alive today, I know what he'd say to the Congress.

He'd say the buck stops right here, on Capitol Hill.

It is the clear duty of the House, through whatever procedures it chooses, to frame a charge of impeachment and to set itself a deadline for the task.

If no agreement can be reached by that deadline, the leaders of the House should tell the American people that no agreed charge could be found.

That is the way to begin to restore confidence.

If a charge is framed and voted, the Senate's clear duty is to proceed to a trial with all deliberate speed.

Since I would be a juror in such a trial, I intend to say nothing in advance about any possible indictment or any possible verdict.

I am not going to call for the President's resignation.

Quite the contrary, I urge the President to do his duty and that is inconsistent with resigning.

Nor am I going to try to fool my constituents into believing that any special prosecutor outside of Congress itself can determine the President's ability or worthiness to govern.

Only the Congress can do that now.

I was reminded recently of the short story Mark Twain wrote called "The Man Who Corrupted Hadleyburg."

Mark Twain hated self-righteousness and in this story he told of how a very self-righteous New England town was brought to grief by a clever outsider who set the town's leading citizens to exposing the frailties and venalities of one another.

Politicians I have known are no greater or lesser sinners than the average person listed in the telephone book.

Nor do I have any reason to believe that the level of sin in our public life is higher than elsewhere.

What bothers me much more are those who now would have us believe that President Nixon and his associates alone are the ones who corrupted America.

It is a truly subversive idea for what would happen if a clever outsider did to us what Mark Twain's hero did to Hadleyburg?

Again I come back to the vital importance of following prescribed procedures.

If the politics of righteous indignation succeeds in persuading the President to resign and relieving the Congress of its clear duty, how long will it be before our politics is corrupted by competitive self-righteousness?

Will it become the accepted fashion to run for public office on the skeletons in your opponent's closet?

Will we after all be corrupted not by real crimes, but by our own incompetence when faced with large issues of justice and morality?

And what will the rest of the world do if we get ourselves in such a state?

Will the word of the United States Government be trusted still?

Or will all other powers try to get something at our expense in every forum they can?

I have spoken before of the grave dangers of moral aggression in foreign policy.

That danger is clear and present now that the feuding families of the Middle East are at war again.

It is a great tragedy because both sides have a legitimate cause.

Israel is fighting for its existence, accepting the sacrifice of another generation of soldiers, against the day when her neighbors will have enough confidence to accept her claim to nationhood.

The Arabs are fighting for that most elemental of all contemporary social needs, the confidence to see themselves as nations, rather than a primitive babble of tribes.

Only a fool would preach the politics of righteous indignation in the face of this grave tragedy.

And that kind of fool is perhaps the greatest threat to the peace of the Middle East today.

Painfully, delicately, against great odds, the community of nations, lead by the United States and, hopefully still, the Soviet Union, are trying to establish procedures that will keep those feuding families from engulfing us all in a third world war.

There being no solution, there only being a hope for a progressive chain of settlements, the procedures become literally a matter of life and death.

Congress's task in following the impeachment procedures set down in the Constitution should be far easier.

The procedures exist.

They don't have to be invented.

But moral aggression here at home is hardly less dangerous than moral aggression in the Middle East.

It threatens to make an epidemic out of the incompetence that the word Watergate has come to stand for.

I hope the leaders of the House of Representatives will rise to their duty.

I hope they will set a deadline, of weeks or months, in which to come up with an impeachment charge.

If the deadline passes without an agreed charge, voted by a simple majority of the House, I expect that the leaders will then tell the American people that no agreed impeachment charge can be found.

If a charge is framed and passed, it is the clear duty of the Senate to initiate a trial with all deliberate speed.

If the President is convicted, so be it.

If not, there will be no legitimate reason for calling for the President's resignation or questioning his right to serve out his term.

As a potential juror in such a trial, I will not have anything to say about guilt or innocence.

None of us was elected to be a megaphone for the loudest voices in our constituencies.

We were elected to legislate and to hold the President and his Administration accountable for their actions.

We cannot afford at this critical time to practice the politics of outraged emotions in carrying out these vital tasks.

Confidence will never be restored that way.

It will only be restored by a determination on our part to follow procedures laid down in the Constitution.

May I now pass on to this Congress advice which I received recently from a fellow Vermonter:

"Either impeach him or get off his back."

RESPONSIBILITIES INHERENT IN A CONSTITUTIONAL DEMOCRACY[5]

EDWARD W. BROOKE[6]

> There is one way and one way only by which the crisis can be resolved, and the country pulled out of the Watergate swamp. I propose an extraordinary act of statesmanship and courage—an act at once noble and heartbreaking; at once serving the greater interests of the nation, the institution of the presidency, and the stated goals for which he so successfully campaigned. That act is Richard Nixon's own voluntary resignation as President of the United States.

These were the words of Senator James L. Buckley, Conservative-Republican of New York, at a press conference in New York City on March 19, 1974. Previously regarded as a "staunch" Nixon supporter, he startled the nation with the boldness of his suggestion. (See *U.S. News & World Report,* April 1, 1974.) One of the stronger rejoinders came from the other New York Senator, liberal Republican Jacob K. Javits:

> I believe it better for the presidency as an institution that its incumbent have the opportunity to respond under the Constitution. . . . Much as I deprecate the necessity for it, I am not afraid for our country of impeachment and trial. I believe the Congress will be fair, that our constitutional processes will stand up, and that . . . our country will emerge stronger and more dedicated to its ideals of freedom and peace than ever before.

A poll showed that Buckley was supported by only one other Republican Senator, Edward W. Brooke of Massachusetts, and fifteen Democratic Senators, some of whom requested anonymity (New York *Times,* March 21, 1974). Brooke had preceded Buckley in his advocacy of resignation; in fact, he made it the subject of a talk that he delivered in Milwaukee on February 27, 1974, to the Associated Students of Marquette University.

[5] Delivered before the Associated Students of Marquette University, Milwaukee, Wisconsin, February 27, 1974. Quoted by permission.

[6] For biographical note, see Appendix.

In that speech, reprinted below, Senator Brooke made clear his purpose when he declared:

> Indeed an educational process is in order to dispel the apprehensions; to correct the misconceptions; and to end the numbing confusion. The time has come to meet head-on the issues of impeachment and resignation. We must remove the clouds of ambiguity that envelop them!

He carefully documented his arguments and presented a persuasive case for resignation. The speech is also a lecture on the nature of impeachment and an appeal for restoration of the balance between the presidency and the legislative branch.

A lawyer by profession, Senator Brooke, the only black Senator, is known as a liberal Republican. He first won fame as the attorney general of Massachusetts, attracting attention as a crime-buster and investigator of corruption in state government. His reaction to Watergate reflects his considerable experience in getting indictments of high-ranking politicians, including a former governor, two speakers of the Massachusetts House, members of the Governor's Council, and a public safety commissioner—as well as individuals and companies that were doing business with the state—on such charges as conflict of interest, conspiracy, bribery, and perjury.

The Senator is articulate, speaks with a well-modulated voice, and is regarded as an effective campaigner.

Impeachment! Resignation!

These headline-grabbing words instill fear in the hearts of many Americans. Sadly they are widely viewed as unthinkable at best and unspeakable at worst. But events propel these terms into the forefront of the American mind and the American vocabulary. And the people of our nation must neither flinch nor falter at their thought or mention.

Indeed an educational process is in order to dispel the apprehensions; to correct the misconceptions; and to end the numbing confusion. The time has come to meet head-on the issues of impeachment and resignation. We must remove the clouds of ambiguity that envelop them!

The events of the past year make it painfully apparent that an extraordinary remedy to the nation's leadership ills must be prescribed. The Watergate revelations have shocked the American people on almost a daily basis. Accounts of criminal misdeeds, unethical conduct, and the attempted subversion of our political processes by members of the President's staff and campaign committee have left America stunned. A chronicling of just the past few months is sufficient to make clear the need for decisive action.

In October, the firing of the first Watergate special prosecutor, Archibald Cox, and the resignations of Attorney General Elliot Richardson and Deputy Attorney General William Ruckelshaus enraged the nation. More than one million telegrams were sent to Congress demanding the impeachment or resignation of President Nixon.

In November it was disclosed that two of the subpoenaed tapes that were the objects of extensive litigation during the summer and the fall did not exist. Shortly thereafter it was announced that a third tape had a mysterious eighteen-and-one-half-minute gap that coincidentally covered the entire conversation between President Nixon and H. R. Haldeman three days after the Watergate break-in.

And then on January 15, in perhaps the most startling revelation of all, a panel of tapes experts, selected jointly by the White House and the District Court, unanimously concluded that the eighteen-and-one-half-minute gap was the result of five, and possibly nine, deliberate erasures.

The Watergate scandal is unprecedented in its scope. Thus far we have witnessed the departure of at least sixteen major Administration officials, including the President's top two White House aides, two attorneys general, and FBI director, and the President's counsel.

In addition, twenty members of the Nixon Administration have either been convicted or indicted for criminal offenses. And it is predicted that major indictments are still to come.

All of this has had a devastating effect on the American people's confidence in their political institutions. And, unfortunately, the nation has especially lost its confidence in its President.

This loss of confidence is reflected in all the polls and surveys. The Gallup Poll of February fourth indicated that 64 percent of those polled do not approve of President Nixon's conduct in office. Those approving dropped to a new low of 26 percent. The latest Gallup Poll shows a slight increase of those approving to 28 percent. And, most alarming is that three fourths of the country believes that the President had some role in the planning or the cover-up of Watergate.

Congress is held in even lesser esteem according to a recent Harris Poll. The poll found only 21 percent of those polled willing to give Congress a positive rating. I believe this reflects the dissatisfaction of the people with a Congress of which members are quicker to oppose than propose and more inclined to rhetoric than action.

One month ago, in his State of the Union Message, President Nixon said that one year of Watergate is enough. In one sense he was absolutely correct—one night of Watergate is too much! But, Watergate and all that has subsequently come under the heading of that umbrella-like word did occur. And, our system of justice cannot rest until the American people have learned the whole truth and those responsible have answered to the law. To accept anything else would be a repudiation of our highest principles.

On November fourth, in response to a question on ABC's *Issues and Answers,* I stated that I had reluctantly come to the conclusion that it would be in the best interests of the country if President Nixon resigned. Ten days later, at a meeting in the White House, I reviewed my thoughts on resignation with Mr. Nixon personally. And, tonight I continue to believe that the President's resignation would serve the best interests of the country.

The reasons for my advocating resignation are many. Most importantly, the President's resignation would spare the country the prolonged agony of impeachment proceedings, trials, and the dreaded prospect of a crippled presidency.

Unencumbered by Watergate and related matters, a new President, in this instance, Gerald Ford, would be able to devote all of his energies to the resolution of our country's problems. He could concentrate on reconciliation and thus eliminate the atmosphere of confrontation that has so consistently dominated the past twelve months.

A significant consideration in my decision has been the effect of Watergate on the Republican party. I have long held that the preservation of the two-party system is vital to the political stability and vitality of our nation. Our two-party system is now threatened more than at any time in our history.

In the past nine months the popularity of the Republican party has decreased at an alarming rate. According to recent polls, in congressional races nationwide, the Democrats were preferred over Republicans by a 58 to 29 margin. Senator Barry Goldwater has released polls that show a 10 percent drop in support for GOP candidates. Most recently in Michigan's Fifth District, held by Republicans since 1910 and by Vice President Ford since 1948, a Democrat was elected over a Republican by a 53 percent to 46 percent margin. And Watergate was the major issue in the campaign. Another indication of the diminishing strength of the Republican party is that no fewer than eighteen Republican Representatives have already announced that they would not seek reelection. And it is difficult, in too many cases impossible, to recruit Republican candidates for the 1974 congressional races.

If this Republican dilemma continues to exist, or worsens, the result would be an unprecedented disaster for Republicans in 1974 and 1976 and thus for the country, which depends on the balance and restraint of our two-party system.

It is for these reasons that I suggest resignation as the

proper course of action. As painful as it may be, and despite obvious difficulties, I believe it to be superior to the alternatives available to us. It offers us the most expeditious means of restoring the confidence of the American people in their governmental processes. It would not be a panacea for our ills, but it would offer us an opportunity to begin anew.

Opponents of resignation claim that it is an extralegal precedent and that it will "destroy the presidency." I believe both arguments are specious.

First, the Constitution explicitly considers resignation in two different sections. Article II, Section I, clearly provides for removal of a President through "Resignation or inability to discharge the Powers and Duties of the Office." The Twenty-fifth Amendment to the Constitution permits the President to resign if he acknowledges that he is "unable to discharge the powers and duties of his office." Obviously, resignation cannot be deemed unconstitutional or "extra-legal."

Other critics of resignation fear that it would mean that future Chief Executives would be hounded out of office when enough voters become disenchanted with them.

But, such critics fail to perceive the essential distinction between this case and those of past and perhaps future presidents. This President is not being asked to leave office because of a fundamental disagreement with his policies and a concomitant slump in the polls. On the contrary, resignation is suggested because President Nixon, based on the misdeeds of so many of his chief subordinates, no longer commands the consent of the governed. In the words of Roger Crampton, the dean of the Cornell Law School, it is doubtful that resignation would set a precedent since in this case there was a "criminal conspiracy emanating from the White House. God help us if it happens again."

But, if, as President Nixon repeatedly suggests, he remains steadfastly opposed to resignation, then we have no recourse but to proceed with the impeachment inquiry in the House of Representatives.

I am not saying that I believe Richard Nixon should be impeached or removed from office. What I am saying is that there is now sufficient evidence before us that warrants, indeed demands, an impeachment investigation. And, we have a constitutional obligation to weigh the sufficiency of evidence as to whether further action is in order.

Americans have an almost preternatural fear of the impeachment process. Raoul Berger, the distinguished constitutional historian, suggests: "Impeachment, to most Americans today, seems to represent a dread mystery, an almost parricidal act, to be contemplated, if at all, with awe and alarm."

Yet, even if, as Lord Bryce once put it, impeachment is the heaviest artillery in the legislative arsenal, it should not instill such unreasonable fear. Though an exceptional remedy, it is not a novel one. The roots of impeachment go back as far as fourteenth century England. Impeachment, said the House of Commons in 1679, was the "chief institution for the preservation of government."

Impeachment is mentioned no less than five times in our Constitution. The Founding Fathers were realists. They recognized the fallibility and weakness of human nature. They drafted a Constitution replete with checks and balances to prevent arbitrary action by any one branch of Government.

Perhaps the remedy of impeachment is the harshest provision in the Constitution. But we must remember that above all else the colonists dreaded a Chief Executive who would exceed the prescribed powers of his office. The impeachment process was to be "a bridle" upon the President, explained the *Federalist Papers,* and it was enacted out of fear of "encroachments of the executive."

Because of the importance they attached to it, impeachment constitutes a deliberate breach in the separation of powers, so that no arguments drawn from that doctrine (such as executive privilege) may apply to the preliminary inquiry by the House or the subsequent trial by the Senate.

And it is herein that I see the greatest portent for a constitutional confrontation, unsurpassed in its enormity and effect. If through defiance or reluctance, the President seeks to impede or thwart the impeachment investigation he may very well find himself subject to impeachment on these grounds alone. I hope, for the nation's and his sake, that President Nixon will cooperate fully with the House of Representatives without any hesitation or qualifications.

The very idea of a presidency kept in check seems startling to many Americans today. Yet, the Founding Fathers were not radicals; it is we who have built up an almost mystical concept of an "Imperial" presidency.

The framers of the Constitution made impeachment and removal an arduous process. It was not designed to be used frivolously. It was meant to be an extraordinary constitutional proceeding whereby a President suspected of committing criminal acts, abuses of power or serious offenses against the public interest could either be exonerated or removed from office. And, that is precisely the situation we face today.

The term *impeachment* itself is often misunderstood. Impeachment is not synonymous with the removal of the President. Strictly speaking, impeachment refers solely to the action of the House of Representatives. When the House decides to initiate an impeachment inquiry, it instructs the House Judiciary Committee to investigate reports or charges of executive misconduct. If the Judiciary Committee determines that the President has committed an impeachable offense it draws up articles of impeachment and reports them to the full House. The House debates and then votes on the articles. If a majority of the House votes in favor of the articles, the President is considered impeached. But this is not a verdict of guilt. Impeachment is more analogous to a grand jury indictment.

The articles are then filed with the Senate, and the

Senate serves them on the accused. The trial in the Senate has the Chief Justice of the United States Supreme Court acting as presiding officer and the Senate acting as judge and jury. A two-thirds majority vote of the Senate is needed to convict. Conviction results in removal from office and a prohibition from running for future public office.

One must concede that the inherent risks involved in pursuing a course of impeachment are real and many. Impeachment proceedings could very well be a long, traumatic, and tortuous experience for the country. Impeachment could cause extreme bitterness and divisions among Americans, leaving the presidency immobilized while it ran its course. And, there is the additional factor that a trial in the Senate resulting in acquittal by slightly more than one third of the Senators would further diminish the President's already gravely impaired ability to govern.

It is necessary to weigh against the risks of impeachment the inescapable costs of a failure to initiate impeachment proceedings. In my opinion avoidance of the impeachment process at this time would have a far more devastating effect upon the fabric of the American body politic than the impeachment proceedings themselves. For their avoidance would mean the relinquishing of one of this country's most precious heritages—the rule of law.

Yet, instead of confronting the disturbing remedies that the Constitution provides, many Americans are willing to tolerate, or ignore, the present situation. They forget Justice George Sutherland's admonition: "If the provisions of the Constitution be not upheld when they pinch as well as when they comfort, they may as well be abandoned."

A recent Roper Poll amply demonstrates this attitude. According to the Roper Poll, almost eight out of every ten Americans believe that the President has committed a serious crime. The poll shows that 45 percent of the people want Mr. Nixon impeached while 44 percent oppose impeachment—but only 11 percent oppose impeachment because they think the President is innocent. The other opponents of impeachment simply fear the destructive impact impeachment might have on the nation.

Other surveys underscore this paradox. One poll shows that the majority of the American people do not want President Nixon to stay on as President of the United States for the next three years. Yet, a very definite majority expect that he will.

These polls seem to say that many Americans have not only lost confidence in their leaders and institutions, but in themselves. How long, I wonder, can our democracy survive the degree of equanimity—or perhaps inurement—that seems so prevalent today? For, if the people are willing to tolerate government lawbreaking, we will cease to have a government of laws.

As Justice Louis Brandeis stated a half a century ago:

> Decency, security and liberty alike demand that government officials shall be subjected to the same rules of conduct that are commands to the citizen. In a government of laws, existence of the government will be imperiled if it fails to observe the law scrupulously. Our government is the potent, the omnipresent teacher. For good or ill, it teaches the whole people by its example. Crime is contagious. If the government becomes a lawbreaker, it breeds contempt for law; it invites every man to become a law unto himself; it invites anarchy.

The American people must not wallow in apathy. And the Congress cannot shirk its constitutional obligations.

And I believe our institutions are durable. Time and time again our country has proved its resiliency. If once more we are asked to prove it, let us go forth and meet the new challenge. Let us not hold back because the way may be difficult. If it is the right thing to do, let us not proceed with undue trepidation, but with the confidence expected of a free people.

The questions of resignation and impeachment, although of crucial importance to the American people, pertain basically to the narrow issues of Watergate culpability and responsibility. It is my hope that whatever the resolution of these issues, we will not ignore the lessons of Watergate.

If Watergate is to have any lasting meaning or significance for the American people, we will have to understand what factors contributed to its inception. Only then will we be able to undertake corrective action and prevent reoccurrences.

Watergate is the result of many complex factors, but perhaps foremost, it represents the culmination of more than four decades of the unchecked expansion of the powers of the American presidency. Beginning with the Administration of President Franklin Roosevelt, we have stood by, helplessly if not happily, as each successive President usurped more and more of the legislative branch's constitutional prerogatives. Congress, by abdicating many of its responsibilities, was an accomplice in this usurpation.

Executive aggrandizement of power has resulted, quite frankly, in the corruption of the Constitution. The careful structural balance upon which the Constitution rests has been uprooted. And few, liberals or conservatives, have done much to prevent it.

The distortion of the Constitution has manifested itself in many areas besides the excesses of Watergate. Two of the more blatant examples are: the power of the purse and the war power. Congress is making progress regaining these powers. We are about to reform our congressional budgetary processes and have enacted the War Powers Act, yet as I previously suggested we remain on a collision course with the executive branch in regard to the doctrine of executive privilege.

Congressional acquiescence, its inability to effectively check the power of the White House had led not so much to the oft talked about arrogance of power, but the power of arrogance. Time and again this arrogance has shown itself in the White House's relationship with Congress, with the judiciary, and with the press.

For too long those in the White House neither feared nor expected a check upon their arbitrary use of power. This aura of impunity no doubt spurred the as yet unknown architects of the Watergate break-in. Sadly, this disdain for constitutional restraints remains even in the wake of Watergate.

If our liberties are to be preserved, if future Watergates are to be prevented, we must search for the means to restore the constitutional balance among the three branches of Government. "Separation of powers" must once again become stern reality rather than a hollow ringing phrase.

And such a constitutional balance, precluding arbitrary actions by any one branch of the Government will mean a Government more conservative procedurally.

Shared and balanced powers and responsibilities are apt to be more slowly applied and upheld. A true balance of power compels increased consultation and compromise. Thus, it entails a less hasty more deliberative governmental pace.

To be sure we often chafe at the sometimes plodding Congress, preferring at times the rapid-fire action which we identify as efficiency, characteristic of the White House. But the framers of the Constitution did not intend for us to remove the keystone of our governmental system—the concept of checks and balances—solely for the sake of efficiency.

To them checks and balances were permanent essentials not temporary expedients. And we must understand that as we seek to reapply these constraints to a President, we thus constrain future Presidents. And these constitutional checks must always be neutral in their application. A popular President or a compelling cause must not at some future time be allowed to vitiate our constitutional safeguards. The lessons of Watergate must be a lasting reaffirmation of the inherent limits and necessary balances of government and above all the inviolable rights of the governed.

This time-tested philosophy applied once again, will insure that ours is a Government carefully and constitutionally defined and limited adherence to this philosophy should prevent future Watergates and restore and renew our constitutional democracy. I know of no more urgent task. I know of no more noble goal.

SPIRIT OF AMERICAN FOREIGN POLICY

STATEMENT TO THE SENATE FOREIGN RELATIONS COMMITTEE[1]

HENRY A. KISSINGER[2]

Under severe attack from many sides, the Nixon Administration has won commendation for its astute conduct of foreign relations. Playing a leading part, Henry A. Kissinger, first as assistant to the President on national security affairs and later as Secretary of State, has carried out difficult negotiations with North Vietnam, China, the Soviet Union, and more recently, with the warring nations of the Middle East. Senator Charles H. Percy of Illinois called Kissinger "a principal architect, with the President, on brilliant and creative foreign policy initiatives that have contributed importantly to the prospects for peace in our time" (*Congressional Record,* September 5, 1973).

Kissinger has made several speeches worthy of inclusion in this volume. Particularly appropriate are those he delivered before the United Nations (September 24, 1973, and April 15, 1974); at the Pacem in Terris Conference (October 8, 1973); and at the Arab-Israeli Peace Conference in Geneva (December 21, 1973). The editor has chosen the statement Kissinger presented on September 7, 1973, before the Senate Foreign Relations Committee. This brief speech carefully sets forth the problems he faced and the positions he proposed to take if confirmed.

The speech should be considered in context. Before being confirmed as Secretary of State, Kissinger, like other nominees of the President, was thoroughly investigated. Over a three-day period, he spent ten hours answering the queries of the sixteen members of the Senate Foreign Relations Committee, including, among others, Mike Mansfield, Hugh Scott, Robert P. Griffin, Stuart Symington, George S. McGovern, Edmund S. Muskie, Hubert H. Humphrey, John Sparkman, and George D. Aiken. After the committee approved the nomination by a vote of 15 to 1 (McGovern voted against confirmation), on September 21, 1973, the Senate confirmed Kissinger by 78 to 7, a vote preceded by a vigorous two-and-a-half-hour debate—one of the bet-

[1] Delivered before the Senate Foreign Relations Committee, Washington, D.C., September 7, 1973.

[2] For biographical note, see Appendix.

ter ones in the Senate this year (*Congressional Record,* September 21, 1973).

In discussing Kissinger's ability, columnist Joseph Kraft has written: "His energy is so great, his capacity to absorb information so large, his instinct for finding the joint of complicated affairs so sure, his manipulative skill so far-reaching that he may just bring it off [the achievement of his goals in foreign relations]."

Kissinger, who has a pronounced German accent (he came to the United States at fifteen to escape Nazi tyranny), is not a brilliant speaker. A description in *Current Biography* (June 1972) notes that "he speaks in a monotone . . . and has a wry and self-deprecating sense of humor." Kraft, however, characterizes his voice as "melodious." With his excellent and precise command of English, he speaks with deliberation, measuring carefully the implications of what he says—a necessary quality for a world diplomat. Whether speaking to the United Nations, reporters, or Senators, he appears calm, unhurried, confident, composed. On camera, he appears jovial, attractive, and disarming.

Mr. Chairman, and distinguished members of the Senate Foreign Relations Committee:

After talking to the Chairman and most members of the Committee, I have the impression that your purposes would best be served if we moved quickly to your questions. Therefore, I shall confine my opening remarks to a statement outlining the attitude I propose to bring to the office of Secretary of State if the Committee and Senate should confirm my nomination. I take this approach, moreover, because the close and cooperative relationship that we shall seek between the executive and the legislative branches in foreign affairs depends ultimately on the spirit with which it is implemented.

My first thought is of the past and the great Americans who have held the office to which the President has nominated me. I derive both inspiration and a sense of gravity from that impressive roster, whether at the dawn of this nation's history—Jefferson, Marshall, Madison, Monroe, Adams, Clay—or just since World War II—Byrnes, Marshall, Acheson, Dulles, Herter, Rusk, Rogers. These men, however different their styles and personalities, epitomized

ditional assumptions need adjustment. We have viewed ourselves as blessed with unlimited agricultural surpluses; today we must contemplate scarcity in relation to world needs. We have assumed self-sufficiency in energy; now we face increasing needs for external supply at least for an interim period. Environmental problems used to be considered national issues, if they were considered at all; now many must be met internationally if they are going to be met at all. We need to explore new conceptual frontiers to reflect the new reality produced by both technology and human aspirations: that our planet has become a truly global society.

This Administration will continue to adapt America's role to these new conditions. But we cannot take for granted what has been begun. We cannot let irretrievable opportunities slip from our grasp. Just as we have benefited from the efforts of our predecessors, so must we build for our successors. What matters to other countries—and to the world—is not so much the work of one Administration as the steadiness of America. So the nation is challenged to render our purposes durable and our performance reliable. This we achieved during most of a generation after the Second World War. We need to continue to do so.

This will require mutual effort and mutual understanding. We will do our part. The President has charged me with helping him to shape a foreign policy that can endure because it is carried in the hearts as well as the minds of Americans.

The first necessity is a broader-based participation within the executive branch. During the last four years, there were many delicate initiatives that required a high degree of secrecy and concentration of effort. Crucial foundations were laid. Now we need to build on these foundations a more permanent structure that we can pass on to succeeding Administrations. Durability in foreign policy is achieved in the final analysis through the deep and continuing involve-

suasion. Our task is to define—together—the contours of a new world, and to shape America's contribution to it. Our foreign policy cannot be effective if it reflects only the sporadic and esoteric initiatives of a small group of specialists. It must rest on a broad national base and reflect a shared community of values.

With good will on all sides, I deeply believe we can reach this goal. There is no dispute about many of the fundamental objectives of national policy. We are at a crucial point of transition in the international order, with major changes in the global structure promising a more peaceful world:

> Successful postwar policies have helped our friends to new strength and responsibilities. We shall work constructively and openly with our partners in Europe and Japan to give new impetus to associations based on shared purposes and ideals. We shall always remember that the vitality of our friendships is the necessary condition for the lowering of tensions with our opponents.
>
> We have developed fresh relationships with adversaries that can ease us away from confrontation toward cooperation. Tensions have been reduced in many areas. For the first time since the end of World War II, all great nations have become full participants in the international system. There is the hope that the arms race can be arrested and the burden of armaments reduced.
>
> Our most anguishing and divisive problem, the Vietnam war, is behind us. We achieved a negotiated settlement last January. The Congress has since expressed its view on how to terminate our military participation in the last area of conflict—Cambodia. As you gentlemen know, the Administration differs with that view. But it will not attempt to circumvent it.
>
> We face unprecedented issues which transcend borders and ideologies and beckon global cooperation. Many tra-

one fundamental reality: that the foreign policy of the United States transcends parties and Administrations. It expresses our ideals, our purposes and our hopes for the world. It must fulfill the best in America.

If confirmed, I shall always be conscious that I hold in trust the legacy of some of our greatest and noblest men.

Let me pay tribute to my predecessor who performed his duties with such dignity and decency for four and a half years. Secretary Rogers headed the Department of State during one of the most difficult periods in our history, when we had to adjust policies to new realities amid major domestic contention. His calm judgment and his humanity helped steer us through this passage and win the respect even of those who disagreed with Administration policies. The President and I will continue to look to him for counsel and support.

Mr. Chairman, we have come to experience in recent years that peace at home and peace abroad are closely related. How well we perform in foreign policy depends importantly on how purposeful we are at home. America has passed through a decade of domestic turbulence which has deepened divisions and even shaken our national self-confidence in some measure. At the same time, profound changes have occurred in the world around us, a generation after World War II. Our era is marked by both the anxieties of a transitional period and the opportunities of fresh creation.

These challenges, though they appear as practical issues, cannot be solved in technical terms; they closely reflect our view of ourselves. They require a sense of identity and purpose as much as a sense of policy. Throughout our history we have thought of what we did as growing out of deeper moral values. America was not true to itself unless it had a meaning beyond itself. In this spiritual sense, America was never isolationist.

This must remain our attitude.

This is why our international policies must enlist the contributions of our best people regardless of political perment of the dedicated professionals of the State Department and Foreign Service, who will manage our foreign affairs long after this Administration has ended. Thus one of my principal responsibilities as Secretary of State will be to infuse the Department of State with a sense of participation, intellectual excitement and mission.

As you know, the President has asked me to retain my position as assistant to the President if I am confirmed as Secretary of State. I believe this will benefit the coherence and effectiveness of our foreign policy. The Secretary of State will be clearly the principal foreign policy adviser to the President. The locus of authority and the chain of authority will be unambiguous. Bureaucratic friction will be minimized. As the President said in announcing my appointment, the unity of position will underline the traditional principal role of the Department of State in the policy-making process.

There must be, as well, a closer relationship between the executive and legislative branches. It is the President's objective to make policy more accessible to the scrutiny and the views of the Congress. This is the fundamental answer to the question of executive privilege. As you gentlemen know, over an extended period of time when I was fully covered by this principle, I met regularly with the members of this Committee, both individually and as a group, and most frequently with the Chairman. I did so partly because I valued this association on personal grounds, but also because of my conviction that this nation faced no more urgent requirement than to promote mutual respect where a consensus was unattainable.

In my new capacity, I shall be prepared to testify formally on *all* my activities. In other words, I shall testify with respect to all matters traditionally covered by Secretaries of State and on my duties as assistant to the President concerning interdepartmental issues. I will not claim executive privilege in either capacity except for the one area customarily invoked by Cabinet officers, that is, direct communications with the President or the actual deliberations of the National Security Council.

We will, of course, need to determine together which subjects should be treated in public and which in executive session.

In short, as a result of my combined position, the Committee should receive substantially more information than it has in the past. We will have acted positively on one of your most central concerns.

This process of greater cooperation will not be confined to formal testimony. If confirmed, I will propose to meet immediately with the Chairman and the ranking member to work out procedures for enabling the Committee to share more fully in the design of our foreign policy.

I will follow a similar approach with the House Foreign Affairs Committee and the leaders of both branches of Congress as well as with other congressional groupings of proper jurisdiction.

This prompts the question, what do we mean by bipartisanship? We do not ask for rubber-stamping and we cannot expect unanimity. Serious people obviously will continue to have differences. Where profound disagreements exist, it would be self-defeating to paper them over with empty formulae. We in turn cannot give up basic principles, nor can we promise to act only when there is bipartisan agreement, though this will be our preference. But we shall work to shape a broad consensus on our national goals and to confine differences to tactical issues. When our views differ, we shall strive not to press the debate to a point that tears the overall fabric of the national consensus. We will seek to maintain a climate of mutual trust so that arguments can center on methods, not motives. We hope that this restraint will be mutual. In this manner, our foreign policy debate can avoid the extremes of civil war and sterile accord for its own sake.

If our foreign policy is to be truly national, we must deepen our partnership with the American people. This means an open articulation of our philosophy, our purposes, and our actions. We have sought to do this in the President's annual reports to the Congress on foreign policy. Equally, we must listen to the hopes and aspirations of our fellow countrymen. I plan, therefore, on a regular basis, to elicit the views of America's opinion leaders and to share our perspectives freely.

Mr. Chairman, I have sketched an agenda for seeking a more durable peace abroad and a cooperative climate at home. Both objectives point to the urgent need for reconciliation. Americans have recently endured the turmoil of assassinations and riots, racial and generational confrontations, and a bitter, costly war. Just as we were emerging from that conflict, we were plunged into still another ordeal.

These traumatic events have cast lengthening shadows on our traditional optimism and self-esteem. A loss of confidence in our own country would inevitably be mirrored in our international relations. Where once we ran the risk of thinking we were too good for the world, we might now swing to believing we are not good enough. Where once a soaring optimism tempted us to dare too much, a shrinking spirit could lead us to attempt too little. Such an attitude—and the foreign policy it would produce—would deal a savage blow to global stability.

But I am hopeful about our prospects. America is resilient. The dynamism of this country is irrepressible. Whatever our divisions, we can rally to the prospects of building a world at peace and responsive to humane aspirations. In so doing, we can replenish our reservoir of faith.

This is our common challenge:

To distinguish the fundamental from the ephemeral.

To seek out what unites us, without stifling the healthy debate that is the lifeblood of democracy.

To promote the positive trends that are the achievements

not just of this Administration but also of those who came before.

To shape new initiatives that will serve not just the next forty months but also the decades to follow.

A few years before he died, one of our most distinguished Secretaries of State, Dean Acheson, entitled his memoirs *Present at the Creation*. He chose that title because he was one of the leading participants in the creation of the post war international system. The challenge before our country now is whether our generation has the vision—as Dean Acheson's did more than two decades ago—to turn into dynamic reality the hopeful beginnings we have made toward a more durable peace and a more benevolent planet.

Mr. Chairman and gentlemen of the Committee, I am confident that working together we can speed the day when all of us will be able to say that we were "present at the creation" of a new era of peace, justice and humanity.

Thank you.

THE ENERGY CRISIS

THE PLANETARY CRISIS AND THE CHALLENGE TO SCIENTISTS [1]

MARGARET MEAD [2]

Watergate stirred much indignation, but the energy crisis touched people directly and painfully. The high price of gasoline, long lines at filling stations, curtailed driving, cold homes, and shortages of petroleum-related products made Americans aware of the seriousness of the worldwide oil shortage and the Arab oil embargo. Who was responsible? Was there really a shortage? What could be done? How long would the shortages continue? These and similar questions provided Margaret Mead with the subject of her talk to the annual meeting of the New York Academy of Sciences, December 6, 1973, held at the American Museum of Natural History, in New York City.

On this occasion, Dr. Mead, one of the most illustrious members of the academy, was elected to honorary life membership, the society's highest award, and was given the sixth annual Lehman Award. Following a reception and dinner, she spoke to about six hundred guests and members in the auditorium of the museum.

In this address, Dr. Mead cleared away many of the misconceptions and much of hysteria associated with the "energy crunch." Placing her appeal on the highest level, she asked her fellow scientists to assume leadership in educating the public. She made her point dramatically:

> This is the first time in history that the American people have been asked to defend themselves and everything that we hold dear *in cooperation* with all the other inhabitants of this planet, who share with us the same endangered air and the same endangered oceans. This time there is no enemy. There is only a common need to reassess our present course, to change that course and to devise new

[1] Delivered before the annual meeting of the New York Academy of Sciences, at the American Museum of Natural History, New York City, December 6, 1973. Quoted by permission.

[2] For biographical note, see Appendix.

methods through which the whole world can survive. This is a priceless opportunity.

Kenneth W. Thompson, acting associate executive director of the New York Academy of Sciences, said that when Dr. Mead finished speaking, "There was a quiet over the hall."

Margaret Mead, curator emeritus of ethnology of the American Museum of Natural History, has been connected with the museum for forty-seven years. She has earned international esteem as an anthropologist, psychologist, teacher, lecturer, writer, and social commentator. There is little doubt that her listeners came eager to gain her special insights into the present crisis, and that she brought to the occasion the lofty ethos that has always added to the impact of her arguments. Three weeks earlier, on November 13, 1973, she had given the Jawaharlal Nehru Memorial Fund Lecture in New Delhi, as a sequel to the Kalingu Award, granted in 1972 for her outstanding contribution to the popular understanding of science. Once again she was carrying out her own admonition: "It is the duty of the scientist to clarify for the public the complex issues."

This is a meeting of members of all the different disciplines included in the New York Academy of Sciences. The members of each discipline are laymen and laywomen to each other. So we meet as scientists, as concerned lay people, and as concerned citizen members of our national and our world communities. But we are gathered together tonight because of our membership in the scientific community. I speak to you as a longtime member of the Academy, and also as a representative of the scientists' information movement represented in the Scientists' Institute for Public Information (SIPI), which was fostered by the New York Academy of Sciences. I am assigning the award money from the Lehman Award which you have given me tonight, to SIPI, to symbolize my adherence to the belief which the scientists' information movement stands for—that it is the duty of the citizen to make major political decisions, but that it is the duty of the scientist to clarify for the public the complex issues which the development of science continually presents today. I speak to you also as an anthropologist who has been honored by the presence of many of my colleagues and by the site of this meeting, the American Museum of Natural History, where I have been a member of the Department of Anthropology since 1926.

The energy crunch, which is being felt around the world —in Japan, in Europe, in the United States—has dramatized for us a worldwide situation and a worldwide opportunity to take stock of how the reckless despoiling of the earth's resources—here in America and all over the world—has brought the whole world to the brink of disaster. It also provides the United States, its citizens, its Government, its scientists, and its leaders of business and labor with a magnificent opportunity to initiate a transformation in our present way of life. Our present way of life was conceived in a spirit of progress, in an attempt to improve the standard of living of all Americans through the increasing capability of technological development to bring previously undreamed-of amenities within reach of the common man. But this search for a better life has—especially since World War II—taken a form which is untenable, and which this planet cannot support. The overdevelopment of motor transport, with its spiral of more cars, more cement highways, more pollution, more suburbs, more commuting, has contributed to the near destruction of our great cities, the disintegration of the family, the isolation of the old, the young, and the poor, and the pollution not only of local air, but also of the earth's atmosphere. Our terribly wasteful use of electricity and of nonrenewable resources are likewise endangering our rivers, our oceans, and the atmosphere which protects the planet.

The realization that a drastic transformation is needed has steadily increased. But the problem has been how to turn around? How to alter our dependence on motor transport? How to persuade the individual citizen enmeshed in a system in which he and his wife and children are imprisoned without one car, two cars, three cars, that change is possible? How to stop building enormous, uneconomical buildings which waste electricity night and day, all year round? How to break the deadlock between environmentalists, bent upon enacting immediate measures to protect an endangered environment, and industry, itself caught in the toils of a relentless compulsion to expand? How to alter our own course and not injure the young economies of the developing countries, desperate to obtain the barest necessities of food and water and light for their hungry millions, clamoring for one percent of our gross national pollution! Even though the present rate of development of energy use and resource use is only some twenty-five years old, it has been so much taken for granted in the industrialized countries that it has seemed almost impossible to turn around short of some major catastrophe . . . some catastrophe which would destroy millions of lives.

The catastrophe has now arrived, not in the form of the death of millions in an inversion over a large city, but in the energy crunch. The causes may be debated, will be debated: how much blame to assign to government mismanagement, how much to the recent war in the Middle East, how much to the action of the oil-producing countries for whom oil represents their only bargaining resource, how much to manipulation by companies that control oil, natural gas, coal, and the processing steps between producer and consumer, how much to the intention of producers to defeat environmental measures, how much to the maneuvers of exporting countries to strengthen their currencies. But in a more basic sense, these triggering events do not matter and focusing on them can in fact divert our attention from a much more important issue—how we are to take advantage of the crisis to move toward a way of life which will not destroy the environment and use up irreplaceable resources, not destroy large sections of the country by ripping off the surface of land in strip mining and by killing rivers, lakes, and the smaller seas like the Baltic and the Barents Seas. We can easily be diverted into acrimonious accusations instead of concentrating on what measures must be taken.

The crisis is here and some kind of crisis activities will

be undertaken. Some measures have been taken. More are underway. But we have the opportunity to use the crisis to transform our own economy, to take the lead in a transformation which is needed right around the world, to aim not for a shallow independence but for a genuine responsibility. We must not be content with half measures, with small, mean palliatives, following the Administration's assurance that all that is needed is fewer Sunday drives to visit mother-in-law and lowered lights on Christmas trees—to be followed very soon by a return to normal waste and pollution. We must not return to complacency over a situation in which our major nutritional disease is *over*nutrition, while millions of Americans are on the verge of starvation and while we are only 6 percent of the world's population, we are using 30 percent of available energy resources. The crisis can and must be used constructively.

During the inevitable disorganization of everyday life, business, industry, and education, we will be taking stands, making decisions, learning new habits and new ways of looking at things, and initiating new research into alternative technologies in transportation, agriculture, architecture, and town planning. It is vital that these activities move us forward into a new era, in which the entire nation is involved in a search for a new standard of living, a new quality of life, based on conservation not waste, on protection not destruction, on human values rather than built-in obsolescence and waste.

As scientists who know the importance of accurate information, we can press immediately for the establishment of an enquiry with subpoena power to ascertain from the energy industries the exact state of supplies and reserves in this country. As scientists, concerned with direction of research and the application of scientific knowledge to a technology devoted to human ends, we can press for a massive project on alternative and environmentally safe forms of energy—solar energy, fusion, other forms. Such a project should be as ambitious as the Manhattan Project or NASA, but there would be no need for secrecy. It would be aimed not at destroying or outdistancing other countries, but at ways of conserving our resources in new technologies which would themselves provide new activities for those industries whose present prosperity is based on oil and motor transport and energy-wasting, expensive synthetic materials.

Those of us who are social scientists have a special responsibility for the relationship between measures that are to be taken and the way in which the American people and American institutions will respond. For example, we have abundant information on the responses of Americans to rationing during World War II. If there is to be gasoline rationing, we have to consider the importance of built-in flexibility and choice. In the United States, a rationing system will only be experienced as fair and just if it discriminates among the needs of different users; recognizes that workers have to get to work, that many people work on Sundays, that different regions of the country will need different measures. Without rationing, we will set one set of users against another, one part of the country against another, encouraging such narrowly partisan measures as severance taxes through which oil-rich states will benefit at the expense of the residents of oil-less states. Rationing is a way of making the situation genuinely national, involving each American in the fate of all Americans.

But while some form of rationing or allotment—or the same procedure by some other name—will be necessary, it will be important to consider that the American people have experienced rationing only as a temporary measure in wartime or as an abhorrent practice of totalitarian countries. There will be danger that rationing may simply accentuate the desire to get back to normal again, with "normal" defined as where we were when the shortage hit us. What we need to do is to define all measures taken not as temporary but as *transitional* to a saner, safer, more human life style. How can we make the present period into a period of tooling up for smaller cars, rapid research, and preparation for entirely new forms of transportation, of utilities, of energy generators? Such mechanisms can be found. In the past, war, revolution, and depressions have provided the dire circumstances within which society's technologies and social institutions have been transformed.

Our present situation is unlike war, revolution, or depression. It is also unlike the great natural catastrophes of the past—famine, earthquake, and plague. Wars are won or lost, revolutions succeed or fail, depressions grind to an end, famine and plagues are over after millions have died. A country rebuilds, too often in the same spot, after an earthquake. The situation we are in is profoundly different. An interdependent, planetary, man-made system of resource exploitation and energy use has brought us to a state where long-range planning is crucial. What we need is not a return to our present parlous state, which endangers the future of our country, our children and our earth, but a movement forward to a new norm—so that the developed and the developing countries will be able to help each other. The developing countries have less obsolescence, fewer entrenched nineteenth century industrial forms to overcome; the developed countries have the scientists and the technologists to work rapidly and effectively on planetary problems.

This country has been reeling under the continuing exposures of loss of moral integrity and the revelation that ubiquitous lawbreaking, in which unenforceable laws involve every citizen, has now reached into the highest places in the land. There is a strong demand for moral reinvigoration and for some commitment that is vast enough and yet personal enough to enlist the loyalty of all. In the past it has been only in a war in defense of their own country and their own ideals that any people have been able to invoke total commitment—and then it has always been on behalf of one group against another.

This is the first time in history that the American people have been asked to defend themselves and everything that we hold dear *in cooperation* with all the other inhabitants of this planet, who share with us the same endangered air and the same endangered oceans. This time there is no enemy. There is only a common need to reassess our present course, to change that course and to devise new methods through which the whole world can survive. This is a priceless opportunity.

To grasp it, we need a widespread understanding of the nature of the crisis confronting us—and the world—a crisis that is no passing inconvenience, no byproduct of the ambitions of the oil-producing countries, no figment of environmentalists' fears, no byproduct of any present system of government—whether free enterprise, socialist or communist or any mixture thereof. What we face is the outcome of the inventions of the last four hundred years. What we need is a transformed life style which will be as different from our present wasteful, shortsighted, reckless use of the earth's treasures as the present twentieth century world is from the agrarian world of the past. This new life style can flow directly from the efforts of science and the capabilities of technology, but its acceptance depends on an overriding citizen commitment to a higher quality of life for the world's children and future generations on our planet.

THE ENERGY CRISIS [3]

Mark O. Hatfield [4]

On March 2, 1974, Republican Senator Mark O. Hatfield of Oregon spoke before the Northwest Regional Conference on the Energy Crisis, meeting at Lewis and Clark College, in Portland. This three-day conference had as its theme "Energy Problems: Crisis or Opportunity?" and was jointly sponsored by Lewis and Clark College, the World Affairs Council of Oregon, the United States Department of Commerce, the Portland Chamber of Commerce, and the Pacific Northwest Regional Commission. Among the 270 persons attending were prominent leaders representing utilities and the petroleum industry, as well as business and consumer groups. In addition to Hatfield, other speakers included George W. Ball, former under secretary of state; John C. Sawhill, then deputy administrator (and presently administrator) of the Federal Energy Administration; Governor Tom McCall of Oregon; Stewart Udall, former Secretary of the Interior; and Irwin M. Stelzer, president of the National Economic Research Associates.

After three days of speeches and panel discussions, the Senator was called upon to address the conference's closing luncheon and hence give the delegates an important final view. He advanced the proposition that "there are certain important principles of how natural forces operate on this planet that we must bring to the attention of our energy planners and our economists" and directed his effort toward making clear just what these principles are. Declaring that the nation was getting "a phony picture" of its energy situation, he discussed the sources of energy and the forces that control it. He concluded with a reassessment of the current explanations of the crisis and offered his own interpretations of them.

The Senator's speaking manuscript is laid out in a sentence-outline form (similar to a debate brief) and in much the same way he might have organized one of his lectures when he was an associate professor of political science at Willamette University. Thus

[3] Delivered before the Northwest Regional Conference on the Energy Crisis, at Lewis and Clark College, Portland, Oregon, March 2, 1974. Text from speaking manuscript. Quoted by permission.

[4] For biographical note, see Appendix.

utilizing the structure and development a college professor might adopt in a lecture to students, Hatfield arranged his presentation under eight headings: introduction, forms of energy, available net energy, energy and economics, energy and ecology, energy and enterprise, energy myths and realities, conclusion.

This speech, in its purpose, organization, and supporting material, is different from many of the speeches published in REPRESENTATIVE AMERICAN SPEECHES. The usual one is either persuasive or inspirational in nature; that is, the speaker strives to change opinion and to get action, or, as in the case of commencement speeches, to strengthen weak and latent attitudes and stir enthusiasm. Hatfield, instead, chose understanding as his primary goal. He did not advocate that his listeners take immediate steps to carry out or advance his recommendations. Rather, he carefully developed his topic from many points of view and offered his interpretation of the forces at work. Not until the last paragraph did he even hint at a prescribed course of action—a course he then presented without any urging at all. He hoped that his listeners would endorse his conclusion that the Government should develop the capacity "to budget according to flows of energy rather than money." Stewart Udall, an authority and frequent speaker on conservation, thought that the speech was the best statement on the subject he had ever heard.

There are certain important principles of how natural forces operate on this planet that we must bring to the attention of our energy planners and our economists. Without the benefit of these perspectives, we will continue reacting only to immediate crises while we rush blindly toward a future that threatens us with energy scarcity, ecological deterioration, and economic disaster. In discussing these principles, we should treat man as the part of the world ecosystem that he is, subject to the same laws of nature as are all other populations of living things.

Man uses energy from many available forms. He consumes food energy in order that the cells of his body may perform their work so that he may function as an organism. He burns fossil fuels—oil, gas, and coal—in order to apply the energy released as heat to fashion certain products for his use or to propel him in vehicles or simply to keep him warm. He converts the heat energy released by the breakdown of fissionable materials to electrical energy, a form he can use to do the same kinds of things he does with fossil fuels. All other living things also use energy, although they are not as proficient at tapping as many different sources as is man.

At the creation of the universe, the energy of the planet earth was the heat of its molten core and the energy locked in the structure of the atoms that make up all matter of the planet. Since that time, other energy forms have accumulated here from the incidence of solar radiation on the surface of the earth. Green plants transformed this solar energy into chemical energy. Our fossil fuels are just dead plant material accumulated over millions of years and converted to their present form by geologic pressures over a period of additional millions of years. They are very "rich" fuels, as concentrations of those millions of years of solar energy conversion by the green plants.

All this fossil-fuel energy that took so long to accumulate we are digging up and burning up in the space of a couple hundred years. Although solar energy continues to arrive at the earth—and it is the only significant source of new energy entering this sphere—it is a very diffuse form of energy. You might have guessed this from the fact that it took millions of years to cause the accumulation of what man is using up in a couple hundred. It is so diffuse that, except for application to heating and cooling buildings, it will be of little use to man for his other endeavors. We must therefore reserve most of our development efforts for the energy that is already right here on earth. And this is no small amount, in gross terms. However, there is a big problem that man is facing with regard to his energy supplies. And that is that the true value of energy to society is not the gross amount that exists in the world. The true value is the net energy—the amount remaining after you subtract the energy costs of getting and concentrating that energy.

Most forms are not concentrated for man's use in technological society. For example, there is easily releasable energy in trees, but we would have to cut down an entire forest and burn the wood in order to get the equivalent amount of BTUs in a single supertanker full of oil. We can concentrate energy from wood by converting it to oil or methyl alcohol, two processes we are now investigating to utilize the wood wastes generated by our timber industry. But we must realize that these processes are costly in terms of the energy that is expended to make the energy of wood available.

The fact that it takes energy to extract energy—to make energy available for our many uses—is a crucial consideration to which our energy planners and economic advisers have not paid attention. We should be asking—and finding out—just how many BTUs are burned up in making ten BTUs of energy available to produce the goods and services we demand. Obviously, if we begin to exploit energy resources that take eleven BTUs in order to make just ten BTUs available, we are going to lose the energy battle. We need to assess the President's "Project Independence" immediately in terms of what we're going to expend for what we intend to get. We need to look at the energy technologies we are going into—coal gasification, extraction of oil from shale rock, nuclear fission reactors, etc.—in this light. But we have not developed the kind of energy accounting system that will allow us to make these assessments.

One thing already appears evident, however. And it is an ominous pattern. These new energy technologies are less and less efficient. It is taking more and more energy to get the energy to make our goods and services. To put it more precisely, the energy that we net from these processes is declining as a percentage of the gross energy released from the source.

The economic ramifications of this development are extremely important. The major new energy processes being developed to replace our conventional sources will require more energy to get the energy available to the consumer. Therefore, they will be more costly to the consumer. You will be paying more and more for the *process* that makes the energy available to you. Consider this pattern:

> In 1965 $1 bought an average of 100,000 BTUs.
> In 1970 the same dollar bought 80,000 BTUs.
> By next year, that 1965 dollar will only get you 50,000 BTUs.

We can soon expect this phenomenon of declining net energy percentage to become the principal cause of inflation, eclipsing all the other inflationary pressures which already are seriously unsettling the US economy.

The more the United States increases its energy consumption under conditions of declining efficiency of the energy extraction process, the more rapidly inflation and the consequent economic instability will increase. An inappropriate energy policy, one that does not take net energy into account, will be felt in terms of a general "economic crisis" rather than in terms of the "energy crisis" that lies at its base. Only when our energy and economic planners recognize this relationship can we begin to attempt an orderly transition, from our present "energy binge," to a period of consumption that is more attuned to the level that our energy sources can support without such adverse economic impacts. The transition will probably need to be accomplished within twenty years, but international political and economic developments could make the need for such a fundamental transition even more urgent.

Further, a national political decision like "Project Independence" if seriously pursued, would also have the effect of hastening the need to control our consumption, as we would begin moving on a crash basis toward implementing expensive technologies that are poor net energy producers—or may even be net energy losers. It could spell disaster for our economic system. I do not deny that technologies such as nuclear fission and coal gasification must be used in the next several decades until something like fusion becomes commercially feasible. We must realize, however, that we cannot possibly afford to consume energy from these sources in the same unlimited fashion that we have consumed the traditional forms of oil, gas, and coal. As we move into this interim period, we must restrain our consumption.

In order to nail down the points I have been trying to make, I would like to discuss some particular details.

We are often presented with statistics about how much oil, natural gas, and coal is still in the ground. These gross figures are then translated into terms such as how many years the United States could continue to run on this amount of fuel. Likewise, projections for the contribution of nuclear power to our energy supply are simply reported in terms of gross kilowatt output. What is ignored in all of this is the concept of net energy.

Suppose that for every ten energy units of some deposit of oil shale proposed as an energy source, there were required nine units of energy to mine, process, concentrate, transport, and meet the environmental requirements. Such a shale reserve would deliver only one tenth as much net energy and last one tenth as long as was calculated using the gross figures. We should be obtaining estimates of net energy from our estimators of energy reserves. We're getting a phony picture today. The net reserves of fossil fuels are mainly unknown, but they are much smaller than the gross reserves which have been the basis of public discussions and decisions that have implied that our present growth can continue unabated.

With regard to our nuclear energy resource, I would estimate that right now it is just barely a yielder of net energy. The high costs of mining, processing fuels, developing and building plants, storing wastes, operating complex safety systems, and operating government agencies make present nuclear power production a marginal operation. Because these supporting operations depend on cheap and abundant fossil fuels, there may not be a major long-range contribution of this nuclear fission technology to our economic survival. I emphasize, therefore, that this is likely an interim technology that will help us through the next thirty-five years or so. When the subsidy of the fossil fuels is removed, this marginal source will be even less economic, and may not be net yielding at all.

Although the breeder process is calculated to increase dramatically the efficiency of fuel use by nuclear reactors, we must be cautious about these figures. They do not show the diversions of other cheaper forms of energy that are required to operate the breeder technology. These diversions amount to an energy subsidy—they support the fancy, energy-consumptive structures and operations that are part of the breeder technology.

The fact is, we do not know whether the breeder will be a better net energy yielder than our present nuclear reactors. Further, this process is being developed near the end of the fossil-fuel era—near the end of the time that fossil-fuel subsidies can help keep the process a net energy yielder.

Many solar energy advocates do not realize that the energy cost of concentrating this form for any use but space heating and cooling is prohibitive, from a net energy standpoint. Forests and food producing plants have already maximized net energy from solar for human use. Plants build tiny microscopic photon receptors that are the same in principle as the solar cells promoted at vastly greater expense by some solar advocates. Such further efforts at concentration of solar energy require large energy subsidies. Plants, on the other hand, build their photon receptors and supporting structures entirely within their energy budget.

This is not to say, however, that some further concentration of solar energy is not possible with reasonable subsidies. Organized agriculture has made higher food (chemical energy) yields possible. Energy subsidies in agricultural efforts include large quantities of fossil fuels for fertilizers and running farm equipment. But beyond agriculture, building solar cells to further concentrate solar energy would be throwing bad money (and energy) after good.

Energy and money are by no means the same, but they

are both currencies which flow through society. Energy is the currency around which we should be basing our economic forecasts, not money supply, the value of the dollar abroad, the value of stocks on the New York Exchange, the price of gold on the world market, etc. In order to get a better picture of where this country is going, or where it ought to be going, we should be thinking in terms of energy. We should develop energy budgets. Energy is absolutely central to our economic life, and this fact alone should show us that if we are to continue to have some control over our destiny, we should start looking at how we use our energy and where we're going to find more on a *net* basis.

Today we are being led to believe that maintaining a quality environment and providing for our energy needs are conflicting objectives. Many of you have seen the advertisements that have appeared recently in our newspapers urging that auto emission controls be junked. Maintenance of our natural ecological systems, however, should not have to compete with man's other uses for energy. These ecological cycles should actually supplement our energy supply, and it is tragic that we have allowed this relationship to be turned around.

We have been making technological choices that have been displacing products and processes which fit in with the cycles of nature. Then, to rescue nature, we have been applying "environmental technology" which substitutes for natural processes, and therefore duplicates the work available from the ecological sector. This displacement and duplication is a crippling economic handicap.

Consider the example of how we handle human waste. As the growth of urban areas has become more and more concentrated, much energy, including research and development work, has gone into developing and implementing technologies to protect our lakes and rivers and coastal waters from the wastes we are dumping into them. These wastes, however, are themselves rich sources of chemical energy capable of being recycled back to the farmlands from which these nutrients came. They would replace much of the fertilizer that we produce from fossil fuels and eliminate the need for energy-expensive tertiary sewage treatment.

When population or economic growth becomes so concentrated that such energy-consumptive technologies as tertiary sewage treatment or automobile pollution control devices start to be employed, then this growth needs to be arrested, or it will arrest itself, through an energy-caused economic depression.

Man as a partner of nature must learn to use well the natural ecosystems. They can be good, cheap recycling processes that utilize the kinds of energy and other resources for which man and nature do not compete. Or they can be destroyed at the same time we're expending great amounts of energy trying to keep them from being destroyed. Our present efforts to resurrect Lake Erie are a good case in point.

Societies appear to compete economically by the same principle that describes how natural living systems compete. The principle is this: Those systems come to dominate that maximize their total net energy from all available sources, and then distribute this energy toward the ends that most promote their survival. In natural systems, a diversity of species develops that allows more of the available energies to be tapped. Many components of such successful systems are specialists in extracting useful power from less concentrated energy sources and they receive subsidies from the richer components of the system.

Consider how trees use energy, for an example of what I mean. The sun-drenched leaves at the top of trees transport fuels that help the shaded leaves get some additional energy from the last rays of dim light reaching the forest floor. Trees use a portion of their rich energies to get a little more energy, even from sources that would not be net yielding alone; thus they develop more total power and more resources for their survival.

In the US economy, we see how our rich fossil fuels have kept all kinds of goods and services cheap, so that marginal energy sources, such as nuclear fission, may receive the subsidy benefit that makes them net yielders. And just as the tree would die if its top leaves were somehow permanently shaded out, our present fission technology may not be able to stand on its own without the subsidy of cheap and abundant fossil fuels.

During times when there are opportunities to greatly expand the net energy available to a society there is a competitive advantage to rapid growth, even to the point of being wasteful of this energy. The last two hundred years of Western culture is testimony to this phenomenon, as Western man rapidly colonized the Americas and Africa and exploited the resources of the Middle East and South Asia. Unfortunately, as we move into a period of declining efficiency in obtaining net energy, Western culture is still locked into a mode of belief that expansion is necessary for survival. Naturally, the Eastern and Third world cultures share this belief and aren't about to be talked into slowing down their development by the Western world.

But at some point soon, man in nature must shift from rapid growth as the criterion for economic competitiveness to a relatively steady state as the model. The timing depends only on whether the breeder reactor works out as a good net yielder. (A later brief reprieve from energy limitations may come if fusion works out.) Man must break out of his expansive ways, which now have him mesmerized, so that his total society can settle into a steady state, just as all other living things must reach an equilibrium point, in balance with the other living things and governed by the constraints of the natural world.

Ecologists have long been familiar with both growth states and steady states, having routinely observed both in all manner of natural systems. For example, they have observed the dog-eat-dog growth competition that occurs every time new vegetation colonizes a bare field. Here the immediate survival premium is first placed on rapid expansion to cover the available solar energy receiving surfaces. The early population consists of weeds that are not as efficient as energy converters, but are fast-growth specialists. Later, these plants are replaced by a population of higher diversity—more efficient in energy tapping, longer living, better controlled, and with more stable components.

Unlike biological scientists, most energy planners and economic advisers have never even conceived of a steady state. They have been trained in their subject during a period of rapid growth. However, most of man's history has been close to an ecological steady state, and it is only the last two hundred years that has seen a burst of temporary growth, because man tapped certain concentrated energy supplies that accumulated over long periods of geologic time. It should be obvious that our most basic assumptions must be reexamined.

I would like to conclude by examining six commonly held, but mistaken, notions about our energy problems.

Myth No. 1: We have unlimited fuel to continue running a highly consumption-oriented society.

We actually have far less net energy in our fossil reserves and in future alternative sources than the gross energies we are reporting. Until we unlock an energy resource that greatly expands net energy yield, our society will suffer greatly if we continue the rapid expansion of the consumer economy that has characterized our last two hundred years.

Myth No. 2: Environmentalists caused the energy crisis.

We must understand that energy is part of the whole realm of creation, and not in competition with it. Our misuse of the natural cycles of the world ecosystem has been our single greatest waste of energy. Not only have we foregone utilizing the energies that power these cycles, we are paying a heavy energy penalty to save these crucial natural cycles from destruction.

At this point, we have no choice but to pay this price. But we need not keep on paying at this rate, if we would only mend our environmental ways in relating to these cycles. Man is an integral part of nature, and it is past time that we should realize the consequences of our acting as though we are not subject to the same natural laws that all other life is subject to.

Myth No. 3: Population increases caused the energy crisis.

The skyrocketing consumption of energy in this country has far outstripped our population increases. Per capita consumption has increased sharply due to the technological choices we have been making. We have been displacing lower polluting, lower energy-consumptive processes with higher polluting, higher energy-consumptive processes:

Synthetic fibers have been displacing natural fibers.
Aluminum and plastics have been displacing forest products.
Truck-freight hauling has been displacing rail.
Aluminum and cement have been displacing steel.
Nonreturnable containers have been displacing returnables.

Consider the impacts:

Synthetics (such as nylon and plastics) accumulate in the environment where they have no place in the natural cycles. They are usually toxic to living systems and cannot be broken down. Their synthesis has heavy power requirements.

Aluminum has ten times the pollution price tag of an equivalent amount of wood. And wood is produced by solar energy in a natural cycle.

It takes six times the energy to move the same amount of freight by truck than by rail.

Production of aluminum, cement, and chemicals consumes 30 percent of the industrial use of electrical power in the United States.
The beverage container industry would consume 40 percent less energy by switching back to returnables.

It is imperative that we cut back on these and other heavily consumptive uses. The displacements I have described came about because of the higher profits inherent in the new processes and it will take economic incentives to get us back on a more ecologically compatible track.

We must stop invading the natural cycles with heavy concentrations of pollutants. In the end these only cause us to use even greater amounts of energy to save ourselves and the world's ecological balance.

Myth No. 4: The energy problem is a temporary US petroleum problem.

The Arab embargo and their price hikes have exacerbated our immediate problem in this country. However, the crucial energy problem—namely, declining net energy yields at a time when man's societies are rapidly developing, growing, expanding—is a world problem. Economic chaos in the more developed Western societies, where the problem will be felt first, will reverberate throughout the world, affecting Eastern societies and the so-called underdeveloped world as well.

Also, as energy forms are closely interrelated, shortages in one form will quickly be felt throughout the various energy sectors. For example, a natural gas shortage in this country soon becomes an oil problem, and the oil problem becomes an electrical power problem as well, as we switch from alternative to alternative energy source.

Myth No. 5: "Project Independence" will solve all our energy problems.

National energy independence, even if it is possible, will not solve the problem of constraints to our net energy output. If anything, Project Independence will bring us more quickly to the day when we must reach that equilibrium position, curtailing our rapid growth pattern and utilizing our net energy wisely, for things that will best serve our economic survival.

Myth No. 6: Traditional economic analysis by the President's Council of Economic Advisers, the Office of Management and Budget, the Federal Reserve Bank, and economics scholars in our colleges and universities will continue to throw light on the central economic problems of our day and guide us safely past the danger of depression.

As I have tried to explain, isolated economic perspectives will not reveal the full dimensions of our economic dilemma. What we tend to see as economic problems will in fact be a net energy predicament.

Only when our leadership is able to grasp the unity of energy, ecology, and economics will we be able to guide our country in the desired direction. Today, instead, we hear adversary arguments coming out of these three disciplines, and this is dangerous to the welfare of our nation and to the role of man as custodian of the earth. In place of the confusion that comes from Western civilization's characteristic educational approach of isolating variables in one-dimensional thinking, we should seek a common-sense overview. Pragmatically, a way to begin would be to set up a capability in government to budget according to flows of energy rather than money. Energy is the all-pervasive underlying currency of our society. We must know how it works, where it comes from, and where it goes. Then we can intelligently deal with it and stabilize the economic fluctuations of our society that are growing wilder every day.

VALUES, RIGHTS, AND LIBERTIES

ETHICS IN PUBLIC DISCOURSE[1]

ROBERT C. JEFFREY[2]

Teachers of communication, whether they concentrate on the oral or written mode, are naturally most concerned about the freedoms protected by the First Amendment to the Constitution and about the good health and ethics of public discourse. They give considerable attention to these subjects in their speeches and publications and at their conventions. The Speech Communication Association, the principal professional association of teachers of rhetoric and public address, has established the Freedom of Speech Commission to serve as a watchdog for the association on these matters. The commission issues two publications: the thrice-yearly *Free Speech Newsletter,* which abstracts important court cases, news items, and speeches; and the *Free Speech Yearbook,* which contains articles on the status of free speech in our society.

It was highly appropriate, therefore, that the president of the Speech Communication Association, Robert C. Jeffrey, chairman of the Department of Speech Communication at the University of Texas, should choose the subject "Ethics in Public Discourse" for his address before his organization's fifty-ninth convention, in New York City, on November 11, 1973. In discussing his choice of subject, he explained:

> The advent of Watergate and the revelation of duplicity among national leaders finally caused me to settle on a speech surrounding that social-political condition. For several years the officers and elected members of the Legislative Council had debated the legitimacy of acting upon resolutions concerning the political affairs of the United States. The decision was consistently made that the Association should not act on resolutions outside of the competence of the members of the Association as teachers and practitioners of speech communication. Consequently, no major resolutions emanated from the Asso-

[1] Delivered before the fifty-ninth convention of the Speech Communication Association, at the Statler-Hilton Hotel, New York City, November 11, 1973. Quoted by permission.

[2] For biographical note, see Appendix.

> ciation relative to the communication atmosphere in the higher levels of government. I personally believe this to be an error, and decided that a position should be stated in opposition to those decisions. It seemed to me that freedom of speech, ethics in public discourse and protection of privacy are directly related to the competence of teachers and practitioners in speech communication. Consequently, I determined to speak on the topic of ethics in public discourse and the responsibility shared by our Association and professionals in speech communication.

Deeply disturbed by Watergate and public apathy, Jeffrey chided his listeners for failing to pass a single resolution which condemned

> the unethical practices of the Nixon Administration for withholding information from the public for political and private purposes; for deliberately deceiving the public with false statements . . .; for refusing to supply tapes, notes and correspondence relating to possible criminal activities; for taping private conversations without the knowledge of the parties being taped; for other acts relating specifically to the free flow of information and privacy of communication.

Jeffrey has written and spoken extensively on public address. Reflected in this speech on the moral decline of official communication practice is his serious study of rhetorical works from Aristotle to present, as well as the deep influence of A. Craig Baird (former editor of this series), who directed Jeffrey's doctoral study. The speech has special import for those in the profession but deserves a wide reading by all who strive to keep free the processes of oral decision making.

Three years ago when I accepted the invitation to be a nominee for second vice president of the Speech Communication Association, I did so as a matter of duty to the Association with little serious thought of being elected. Upon learning of my election, I was forced to contemplate the rigors of the offices suddenly thrust upon me. Contemplation led to the realization of a commitment to edit the convention abstracts, the principal duty of the second vice president, and to plan the national convention, the principal duty of the first vice president. These onerous chores could be endured, I concluded, if the thought of the presidential year were kept foremost in mind. I discovered that editing the convention abstracts was not as onerous as I had anticipated, and that planning the convention can be both pleasurable and rewarding, as well as time-consuming. I have discovered more importantly, in the three years of official service to this Association, that accepting the demands of professional activity has proved, ultimately, to be its own reward.

Last December, with the first two years of service completed and Ted Clevenger's term approaching closure, I turned to the *Operations Manual* of the Association for assistance in performing the duties of the president. On the page titled "Guide for Presidents," Don Bryant stated one procedure succinctly: During the summer and fall of the presidential year, "the president should compose an *excellent* presidential address for the national convention of such scope as the president thinks fit." He further advised: "Try out parts of it at regional and other meetings." The platform you provide me as president of the Speech Communication Association is a hearty source of professional satisfaction and, taking Don Bryant's admonition seriously, one I would like to capitalize on today in discussing a much-neglected concept in the teaching and research in communication—the problem of ethics in public discourse.

Many of you at regional or state conventions have heard me refer to several events and practices in our world today that threaten our ethical communication conduct. One of those practices is the employment, with tax monies, of an "executive flunky," if you will, as a mouthpiece for the President of the United States. Mr. Ziegler in the present Administration holds this post. As communication strategists we have passively and uncritically accepted this practice, thereby harboring and condoning the institution of a "presidential scapegoat," an institution that permits our highest elected officer to test public opinion in a quasi-official fashion. If reaction to the statements attributed to the President is negative the President can deny responsibility for the statement. With this simple mechanism of public statement by proxy we encourage both deliberately designed deception and abrogation of responsibility.

By permitting our highest elected officials and those they appoint to administrative posts to classify information as confidential, and by placing no constraints on those public servants, we deny the public information necessary for proper decision making in the democratic process. Equally as reprehensible and deplorable is our national Administration's malfeasant efforts to weaken the integrity of the press by deliberate design. At this convention last year, New York *Times'* writers Robert Semple and James Naughton concluded that the present Administration has been so successful in undermining the credibility of the press that the public refused to acknowledge the Watergate saboteurs once exposed. That, of course, was prior to the Watergate hearings. The word *cover-up,* however, has now become a household word and extends beyond the Watergate matter to areas perhaps yet to be discovered.

These practices are among many that lead inevitably to the conclusion that the American public refuses to demand an ethical responsibility from its leadership. It is a frightening prospect, and one that Richard Nixon viewed with alarm in 1970 when, recalling the bombing at the University of Wisconsin in that year, he said, "What corrodes a society even more deeply than violence itself is the acceptance of violence, the condoning of terror, excusing of inhuman acts in a misguided effort to accommodate the community standards to those of the violent few."

If we substitute the words "crime" or "irresponsibility" for the word "violence," we arrive at the basis for my remarks this afternoon.

The corrosive effect of the acceptance of deception has led to the cheapening of authority in America in recent years. Too many broken promises, too many empty words, too little real achievement of vital objectives, too many inept or insensitive or inexplicable decisions made by untouchable officials in unreachable institutions—all of these have undermined both the integrity of and our respect for the figures who lay claim to executive leadership and executive "privilege." This disintegration of administrative morality and accompanying public impertinence extend beyond the American presidency to leadership in the universities, corporations, unions, and organized religion. Some of the practices of our profession have, in my opinion, contributed, however subtly, to this impalement of national morality.

First, the research emphasis in human communication has, for over a decade, been behaviorally oriented, accompanied by an abandonement in many academic programs of a healthy and balanced orientation with interest in humanistic and ethical aspects of communication. Historically, technological progress has always left in its wake agonizing political and social change, and even though earth's complexion has changed every minute since it first took off around the sun, what is so shockingly new about our changing world is that where it once changed imperceptibly, it now convulses and heaves and shatters and reconstitutes itself before our very eyes. Reflecting this scientific upheaval is the behavioral and objective orientation in communication research in which the *human* as individual is often neglected and the *mass* as individual is subjected to experimentation and manipulation.

We have been "scientifically" aware, however, since the turn of the century that no objective reality exists, that every perception of objectivity, regardless of the sophistication and precision of our measuring instruments, in the final analysis, is determined by individual perceptivity and capability. It is amazing that since Planck's discovery of Quantum Theory in 1900 the "scientific" world has recognized the reciprocity between the scientist as individual and the world he seeks to control, and yet, we in speech communication are propagating as "new," "progressive," and "innovative" a view of human behaviors strangely reminiscent of nineteenth century scientific thought.

Related to the emphasis on scientific investigation of communication behavior is a second practice contributing to the ethical and moral decline in our communicative society—an extreme concern with the development of images in leadership roles. As Daniel Boorstin so eloquently put it, "The making of illusions which flood our experiences has become the business of America." The sophistication of contemporary illusion *making* results from the subjugation of individual identity to group profile, inevitably leading to excesses in promoting products for human consumption and images for leadership roles. Encouraged by such falsified profiles of human behaviors, experimentation on changing human behavior on the basis of group norms rather than individual reasoning has become paramount. If, in persuasion, there were more concern for the integrity of the individual, there might be less need for truth-in-lending laws, truth-in-advertising laws and fairness-in-campaign-practices legislation.

In speech criticism, our research and publications reflect a near obsession with tracing the development of images in political campaigns, resulting in an abrogation of our responsibility to students and the public. We no longer demand accuracy of statement, and too often train our students to be experts in the art of plotting the creation of deceptive practices rather than unmasking and indicting those practices. The loss of respect for the spoken word, an inevitable product of image making, has led former Attorney General John Mitchell, referring to the Nixon Administration, to assert, "You will be better advised to watch what we do instead of what we say." This statement led Richard Harris, in his book *Justice,* to remark that the statement was "the most astonishing admission of high-level duplicity in government history."

A third practice of teachers and researchers in communication that has contributed to the lack of concern for ethical and moral responsibility on the part of American leadership is our growing preoccupation with the *superficial* dimensions of nonrational discourse, body rhetoric, the rhetoric of the streets, the rhetoric of numbers. Wayne Booth, recognizing both the rhetorical validity of such acts of persuasion and their inherent dangers, asserts, "A case could be made for the claim that we live in the most rhetorical age of all time, if by rhetoric we mean whatever men do to change each others minds without giving good reasons for change." Booth's extension of what constitutes rhetoric demands a return to an ethical consciousness.

An integral part of a new rhetorical theory must be a renewed consideration of ethics in public discourse. This consideration must of necessity revert to a discussion of Aristotle's determinants of a moral act. Father Lawrence Flynn succinctly describes the Aristotelian determinants of a moral act in a 1957 article in the *Speech Teacher*. He reasons first that a moral act is dependent upon the establishment of a human act. He writes,

> A truly human act proceeds from a rational agent who knows what he does and chooses freely to do it. The power to reason, which distinguishes men from brutes, underlies man's recognition of a means-to-end relationship. So, before we choose means-to-end we must know the end, the means, and the relation between them. To perform human acts we need knowledge and human choice.

To determine the goodness or badness of a human act, however, requires an analysis of the object, the act, the intent of the agent, and the circumstances surrounding the act. Consequently, in determining the ethics of a public statement, it is necessary to analyze what the speaker does, why he does it and the circumstances under which he does it. The measurement of effects of a public utterance may offer historical fact, but reveals nothing of the utterance's ethical structure. Even though the speaker's purpose or ultimate end is good, Aristotle would require that the rhetorical devices, techniques, methods, or fact pass the test of morality according to the three determinants. If the end sought by the speaker is good, the act of achieving that end is unethical if the speaker selects unethical means. Likewise, even though means to achieve an end are ethical or good, the end itself may be bad. Consequently, to judge the goodness or badness of a speech or other communicative act, all of the determinants must be satisfied. Deliberate falsification is morally faulty because it frustrates the natural purpose of speech in a democratic society which is to transmit judgments to auditors, and because it interferes with the auditors' judgment capabilities.

Since the human act, to be judged morally, must be deliberate and free, one might suppose that an unconscious misrepresentation or falsification that may result in a partial distortion or complete misrepresentation through ignorance would be excused. However, a speaker must assume the responsibility for his statements and, consequently, do all that is possible to remove his ignorance before making the statement. Ignorance cannot be claimed as an excuse unless it can also be shown that the speaker did what was within his power to remove that ignorance. Father Flynn would have us ask the question, "Did he use care proportionate to the importance and gravity of the situation?"

It has been, and can be argued that the logical and emotional aspects or rhetoric are amoral, that they derive their morality from the good or bad intent of the speaker or agent. The use of logic in a particular discourse may be bad, but it is not morally bad unless the intent of the user is bad. The problem, then, is to determine the intent of the communicator or agent.

Often it is possible to determine the intent of the agent by the arguments assembled in the message. For instance, most rhetorical critics would consider Nixon's 1952 "Checkers Speech" logically unacceptable as a defense for misusing campaign funds. Few, however, have questioned the ethical base of the speech or the morality of the act. The general public response to the speech then, as now, lauded it as a monumental rhetorical effort. This kind of critical acceptance justifiably places the term rhetoric in dubious quarters.

Much to his credit, Barnet Baskerville wrote in his analysis of the vice presidential speaking in the 1952 campaign that the "Nixon affair" served to unify a divided Republican party and elevated Richard Nixon to a prominence seldom enjoyed by a vice presidential candidate. He also observed,

> It seems to this observer that the phenomenal public reaction to the original charge, to the speech itself, and to subsequent countercharges, revealed an alarming preference to appearances rather than realities, a widespread preoccupation with legality rather than morality, and a subordination (by Democrats and Republicans alike) of ethical considerations to political expediency.

The period of the early 1950s might well serve as the reference point for the beginning of the deterioration of responsible public discourse in the high levels of government. Hal Gulley wrote in *Today's Speech* in 1970, that "America's public statement making is less dependable, reliable, and candid than it was two decades ago; that we are witnessing a national drift toward irresponsibility toward public utterance. In some areas of our national life, we cannot now be certain that we believe what some people are saying." Gulley's report contained an alarming exposure of the cavalier attitude with which government officials view high-level duplicity. He quoted former assistant secretary of defense for public affairs, Arthur Sylvester, as saying, "It is the Government's inherent right to lie if necessary to save itself when faced with nuclear disaster; this is basic."

We as a nation in 1973 have been brought to the brink of moral and ethical deterioration in our government. No one in this audience needs be reminded of the general and pervasive political debauchery associated with the amorphous term Watergate. Testimony of men respected for their place in Government has revealed the exalted place of the lie and of deceit. James Reston wrote in the New York *Times:* "Future testimony from Messrs. Mitchell, Ehrlichman, Haldeman, and Dean may throw more light on who is lying and who is telling the truth. Meanwhile, it is probably better to follow Paul Porter's skeptical advice: 'I don't say these men are liars, . . . it's just that they have such respect for the truth that they use it sparingly.' "

In this time of national despair and uncertainty, we should not neglect to celebrate the system of justice that has revealed the unethical conduct of some of our more respected leaders. Our system of justice may be slow in its process, but it offers assurance of ethical certainty in its results.

The real question, however, is not whether the guilty will vindicate the innocent. The question is, rather, "Where lies the culpability for having arrived at this near disastrous condition?"

Every man, a President included, must be accountable for his acts and responsible for his statements. But if the President acts or speaks irresponsibly, those who elected him to office are not free of guilt if the evidence of irresponsibility was available at the time of election. Richard Nixon's questionable ethics have been observable for over two decades. But in those two decades, academic critics and scholars in communication have been more concerned with the technologies of communication than with its ethics. Richard Nixon was and continues to be a "technician" in manipulating public attitudes for self-aggrandizement. Our own publications reflect a preoccupation with Nixon's predictability, his appeals to audiences, his mastery of the television medium, and so on. Few articles, however, have analyzed the ethics or morality of his statements. It is a sad commentary on the state of rhetoric in the academy when we admit that ethical studies of the Nixon rhetoric are more readily available in the press than in scholarly journals. Traditionally, rhetorical critics have, in fact, recognized and accepted their charge as analysts and reporters of ethical conduct. The fourth estate, however, and not rhetorical scholars, first alerted the American public to Nixon's special brand of administrative rhetoric. Kenneth Burke has used the term "administrative rhetoric" to explore the ethical dimensions of Machiavelli's *The Prince.* He contends that

> Machiavelli's *The Prince* can be treated as a rhetoric in so far as it deals with a producing of effects upon an audience. Sometimes the prince's subjects are his audience, sometimes the rulers or inhabitants of foreign states are the audience, sometimes particular factions within the State. If you have a political public in mind, Machiavelli says in effect, here's the sort of thing you must do to move them for your purposes. And he considers such principles of persuasion as these: either treat well or crush; defend weak neighbors and weaken the strong; where you foresee trouble, provoke war; don't make others powerful; be like the prince who appointed a harsh governor to establish order . . . ; do necessary evils at one stroke, pay out benefits little by little; sometimes assure the citizens that the evil days will soon be over, at other times goad them to fear the cruelties of the enemy; be sparing of your own and your subjects' wealth, but be liberal with the wealth of others; be a combination of strength and stealth (the lion and fox); *appear* merciful, dependable, humane, devout, upright, but be the opposite in actuality, whenever the circumstances require it, . . . in order that you may get the advantage of good advice without losing people's respect, give experts permission to speak frankly, but only when asked to speak; have a few intimates who are encouraged to be completely frank, and who are well-plied with rewards.

Each of us can find specific instances of these administrative rhetorical strategies in the Nixon speeches. They are identifiable as early as 1948 when, in his senatorial campaign, he goaded the public to fear the cruelties of the enemy and assured the voters that the fear would end with his election. The strategies are even more identifiable today with the crumbling of popular respect for the man and his rhetoric.

As communication critics and educators, we failed in our responsibilities to officially oppose those practices when they became so blatantly evident. We persist in that failure today. In the ten hours of deliberations of the Legislative Council at this convention, not a single resolution was introduced to condemn the unethical practices of the Nixon Administration for withholding information from the public for political and private purposes; for deliberately deceiving the public with false statements as in the denial of bombing in Cambodia when, in fact, it occurred; for refusing to supply tapes, notes and correspondence relating to possible criminal activities; for taping private conversations without the knowledge of the parties being taped; for other acts relating specifically to the free flow of information and privacy of communication that should be the central concerns of teachers and scholars in speech communication.

This temerity in speaking to the corrupt communication practices of the present national Administration reveals an abrogation of our role as protectors of ethical communication. If there is one thread that binds together all of the varied interests in our association, it is a dedication to free and responsible speech. Yet, when that freedom and responsibility is abridged or threatened, we fail to act. In this case, the excuse that we must act only in areas of professional competence cannot be claimed as a defense by those who would oppose censure resolutions by this association.

Last year, at this convention, the Legislative Council passed a resolution declaring that

> it is the role of the Speech Communication Association, defining itself as a humanistic organization, to be concerned with the communication process and how that process affects human beings; that since those in political power make decisions affecting millions of people, those people have a right both to know those decisions and to offer information and well-considered opinions on them; that in the past it has been apparent that government plays a substantial role in determining the limitations of freedom of speech and the amount of information made

available to the public; and that there is a need to study government use of communication, whether it involves abridgment of free speech, failure to communicate to the electorate, or responsible use of communication channels.

With this expression of concern for government's use of communication controls, our purpose should be to monitor it and to condemn or praise as the case may warrant.

It may well be true that the moral and ethical permissiveness of the present Administration has, as Russell Baker wrote, so accustomed us "to accepting mendacity as a normal condition of life that we assume it is natural for everybody to lie to us, even our best men." But ethical permissiveness, even in a just cause, corrodes the soul; and condoning it can corrode a nation. As Adlai Stevenson once asserted, "Those who corrupt the public mind are just as evil as those who steal from the public purse."

As teachers and scholars in communication, our purpose should be to develop respect for ethical communication and a healthy disdain for deception in and corruption of public discourse. Henry Wieman and Otis Walter wrote in 1957, "Ethical rhetoric has the promise of creating those kinds of communication which can help save the human being from disintegration, nourish him in his growth toward uniquely human goals, and eventually transform him into the best that he can become." That should be our paramount goal as teachers and scholars in communication.

"FREE JUST FREE"[3]

WES GALLAGHER[4]

> Congress shall make no law respecting an establishment of religion or prohibiting the free exercise thereof; or abridging the freedom of speech, or of the press; or the right of the people peaceably to assemble, and to petition the Government for a redress of grievances.—The First Amendment to the Constitution

The First Amendment is regarded as the touchstone of our freedoms. Even a slight threat to the mass media is likely to produce a vigorous reaction. Often, however, the words are hollow. As Representative Charles W. Whalen, Jr. (Republican, Ohio), says:

> For nearly two hundred years Americans have pontificated about the necessity of the First Amendment in a free society. Yet, despite our rhetoric, First Amendment values still do not occupy a preeminent position in our society. With all the glowing phrases spoken about the First Amendment and the respect we ostensibly accord to the concepts embodied therein, the freedoms it guarantees have come under constant attack—and by decent, law-abiding citizens as well as by government officials.

Since 1969, with the advent of the Nixon Administration, the owners and representatives of mass communications media have had cause for alarm. The public pronouncements of President Nixon and former Vice President Agnew, the failure to hold presidential press conferences, the Pentagon Papers episode and the Ellsberg trial, the threatened use of the subpoena power to unmask a reporter's confidential sources, numerous court cases involving reporters and broadcasters, the questionable editing of television scripts and tapes by network personnel, dissatisfaction with the Fairness Doctrine, and the attempted cover-up of the Watergate affair—all these have stirred frequent edi-

[3] Delivered at the thirty-seventh annual Press Day, at Saint Bonaventure University, Saint Bonaventure, New York, May 14, 1973. Previously published *LSU Alumni News*, September 1973, p. 608. Quoted by permission.

[4] For biographical note, see Appendix.

torial comment, numerous commentaries, and many speeches. This climate provided Wes Gallagher, president and general manager of the Associated Press, with the subject matter of his speech "Free Just Free," delivered on May 14, 1973, as the main address at the thirty-seventh annual Press Day, sponsored by the Department of Journalism of Saint Bonaventure University. His audience was composed of 2,500 high school and college students associated with scholastic and collegiate publications in several states, and 100 professionals from the various mass media. A widely known institution, Press Day was especially attractive because some 750 incentive awards for excellence were made to students. Throughout the day-long program, seventy-five journalists lectured and chaired workshops. Among them were William C. Payette, president of United Feature Syndicate and at the time president of Sigma Delta Chi, the professional journalism society; and Peter Bridge, the New Jersey reporter who had been jailed for twenty-two days for his refusal to reveal a confidential source to a grand jury. Others included broadcasters, editors, reporters, and press photographers.

Unlike the more militant defenders of the mass media, Gallagher presented a tempered statement on the role of the press—its freedom, its power, its responsibility—in a balanced society.

Ladies and gentlemen, it is not usual to begin a speech with a quotation and I would like to do so today to make a point.

It also perhaps proves that I can read and do so occasionally.

But to the quotation:

"We find a notorious scandalous paper called the *Courant,* full of freighted nonsense, unmannerliness, raillery, prophaneness, immorality, arrogancy, calumnies, lyes, contradictions and what not all tending to . . . debauch and corrupt the minds and manners of New England."

Now this was not our good friend, the Vice President [Spiro T. Agnew], the present-day master of alliteration, but another man who knew his mind—Cotton Mather, in 1721.

I cite this merely to show the struggle in this country over the press predates even the Revolution.

The battle over the role of the press in our republic

is not new but it certainly is more shrill, acrimonious and complex today than it ever has been.

There are those Cassandras who see a free press as doomed. Others would like to see it restricted in a society growing increasingly controversial and disturbing to their peace of mind.

But there never has been a time when a free press was more essential to the maintenance of your personal freedom.

Let us examine why this is so.

The founders of our country were suspicious of power —any kind of unrestrained power. They had lived under King George and his colonial governors and had seen their freedoms trampled on to the point where they revolted—a revolution incidentally that started with very small chance of success. They had seen tyranny, thievery, misconduct and misjudgment in high places.

This was a nation of militant refugees escaping the despotism of an oppressed Europe.

When the time came to write the Constitution this suspiciousness was deep in the American soul and was reflected in how the founders set up a government of checks and balances.

A president who could speak on behalf of the nation; but a congress which would make the laws that he would put into effect.

Then an independent judiciary that would make sure that neither Congress nor the President exceeded the powers granted by the Constitution or infringed on the freedoms of the individual.

Then a free press to watch the activities of all forms of government and report to the people—a fourth estate.

The Constitution reads "freedom of the press" without adjectives or restrictions.

Free to speak with a multiplicity of tongues.

Free to give voice to any criticism.

Free to print the ideas of minorities.

Free to criticize those in power.

Free even to make mistakes, then to be checked by libel laws so the individual citizen is protected.

A government of checks and balances.

Would it be so if there were no press?

Who would know if power were usurped by any arm of Government? Who would know of the clandestine activities of the Ku Klux Klan? Of injustices in the courts? Of Teapot Dome? Of wheat deals? Of Watergate? Who would report the infringement on individual freedoms?

Would the nation have known how badly things were going in Vietnam? Not from the Government, as the Pentagon Papers show. It was the press that told the public the facts about the war long before the Pentagon Papers themselves were published. The journalist cost was heavy, for Vietnam claimed the lives of four Associated Press reporters alone and over its long course the lives of thirty-nine newsmen and newswomen since 1965 alone.

Watergate. Would it have ever come to full light without the investigative zeal of the Washington *Post* and a number of other papers, plus the inquiry of an aroused Congress and the deep suspicions of a courageous judge who felt he was not being told the full story?

A perfect example of the checks and balances built into the Constitution, at work nearly two centuries after it was written.

I wonder if the framers of the Constitution realized how wisely they had built for the future? I wonder, too, if they should be able to return to earth today, would they still be suspicious of the enormous power big government has to regulate people's lives? I suspect they would.

But they did build a system of government of checks and balances that has lasted nearly two centuries while other republics have come and gone, dictators have come and come again, and again and again, and scores of compromise governments, almost all with unchecked strong executives, have fallen in bloody revolutions.

The key to our success in self-government lies in maintaining the delicate balance of a functioning executive branch, an active Congress, an independent judiciary and a free press.

It gives this republic a flexibility to absorb the bad news and good news and the blows of an increasingly complex civilization which toppled less flexible governments.

Under the pressures of a long unpopular war there were those who felt this balance was being destroyed: that Congress was becoming a rubber stamp for executive Government, that the judiciary was being politicized and that the press was being weakened under heavy Government criticism plus attacks by the young who distrusted the press as a member of the Establishment.

Now the pendulum has started to swing back. Congress is aroused over what it feels is the usurping of its power by the executive branch of Government. Judges in Los Angeles and Washington have challenged major Government prosecutions.

And there are those who feel that the revelations of Watergate have in a large measure restored the credibility of the media and underscored the necessity of a free press to watch over the government.

So it has temporarily. The Government critics either are silent or their protestations over the truth of news stories have a hollow ring.

But these are but scrimmages and temporary victories in a struggle that will go on as long as the republic stands. If it ever stops we no longer will have a free society.

For there are those individuals and groups in every society who seek power at the expense of others or would substitute their views to the exclusion of those of their opponents. And, there are those who yearn for a simpler time and less controversy and just wish everyone would be silent.

But there is always a price to pay for your freedom and it was expressed by Thomas Paine in these words: "Those who expect to reap the blessing of freedom must undergo the fatigue of supporting it." This is more true than it ever was.

And in that lies the challenge to you young people who are interested in journalism.

The problems of supporting a free press, print or broadcast, grow daily, but so do the opportunities.

In this profession of journalism you can take satisfaction in maintaining an essential part of a free society. Without a free press we would live under dictatorship. It is a fundamental right of the people to know what their government, elected officials and courts are doing, or perhaps more important, not doing.

You should recognize, too, that if you do your job well you will not be popular. The reporters in Washington writing of Watergate win few plaudits from Government officials. The reporters at Wounded Knee, writing that a small group of Indians contrived this confrontation which resulted in two deaths to seek publicity, will win no medals from militant minorities.

But you will have deeper satisfactions than popularity for a journalistic job well done—the task of defining complex problems of the day, and by so doing lead to their solution by the public.

In recent years the Government has been making the job more difficult with subpoena actions and court actions ranging from the serious to the ridiculous.

The Reporters' Committee for Freedom of the Press lists sixty-seven separate court actions taken against reporters and editors either by Government or defense lawyers, seeking reporters' notes, sources or asking for restraining actions of various types.

This is more than at any one time in our history and stems from a number of causes. These causes include lazy prosecutors seeking to use the press to do its work, defense attorneys devoid of ideas seeking the same end as prosecutors, judges irritated by critical press reports, Government officials seeking to retaliate against the news sources of stories they did not like and perhaps most of all the climate of the times.

It is an immutable law of journalism that: Attacks on the press by government rise in direct proportion to the amount of adverse news printed or broadcast; and criticism of the press by the public rises in direct proportion to the amount of news read which undermines what it would like to believe, whether true or not.

There are many ironic contradictions in these attacks on the press, both print and broadcast.

The government seeks to force reporters to disclose their sources but the acting director of the FBI, L. Patrick Gray 3d, testifying on the Watergate case said: "People will talk to the FBI . . . but they will not continue to do so if we continue to spread this information on the public record."

This is precisely the reporter's dilemma—if he is forced to make public the names of his sources, news will dry up.

There are some in government who want the names of reporters' sources for the very reason the reporter must protect them—the government wants to take retaliatory action against the sources to silence them.

There is no easy solution to this problem of news sources and I doubt very much that a Federal shield law will be passed, or that in seeking one we are wise.

I am reminded that in the flush of victory in World War II, the United States sponsored a United Nations document to insure free access of information on a worldwide basis. After years of debates and amendments by various governments the press of this country had to ask the United States to kill the resolution because so many restrictions had been written in it that would make the situation worse than it was.

The same thing can happen to Federal shield legislation.

And, may I point out again that the Constitution is devoid of restrictive adjectives—it simply says the press shall be "free." It is hard to improve on that.

It seems to me that the only long-term solution is to fight out each case in the courts even though some courts seem hostile at the moment.

There is no doubt this will be a long, tough process and before it is over some reporters, editors and publishers may have to spend some time in jail building up legal precedents. Some of you in this audience may have to fight this battle.

Harassment of the press will only stop when the press itself proves the futility of such steps.

It seems to me the question of reporters' notes is far less serious. I have never met a reporter yet who could make head or tail of his notes a week after he had written them and if there were anything important in them it should have been in the story in the first place.

In any case, if there is any challenge as to ownership it should be met and fought by the employer.

The view that the press must fight its own battles was expressed by Judge Harold R. Medina, who pointed out that serious violations of the First Amendment are frequently committed by the courts "in the complete muzzling of the news media, lawyers, law enforcement officers and everyone else."

Judge Medina added:

> Some people may think that leaders of a free press would perhaps accomplish more if their claims of constitutional rights were less expansive. I do not agree with this. I say it is their duty to fight like tigers right down the line and not give an inch. This is the way our freedoms have been preserved in the past and it is the way they will be preserved in the future.

Now young people like yourselves are usually idealists willing to make sacrifices. What better profession could you have than the one I have sketched, where you will be: unpopular, criticized by your friends and may have to go to jail—all for the public good.

More seriously, in closing, may I point out again the vital necessity for a strong role by the journalist in our society.

The Founding Fathers did not create a free press by accident. They had learned their lessons through the jailing of Peter Zenger and others. They viewed a free press as equal in importance to Congress and the courts.

With that important role for the journalist goes a heavy responsibility to be fair and accurate in his work.

Mistakes will be made because we are human and in the rush of news will make them. But when we do we should be the first to correct them, without waiting for others to do it for us.

We should remember, too, there is power in a free press. Like all power it must not be abused or misused. We need more investigative reporting, more news on behalf of the individual lost in a computer society, but we cannot afford to slip from investigator to prosecutor in a blind zeal to reform. That is the role of the judiciary in our balanced society. If we abuse the power of a free press the pendulum today swinging in the press's favor will swing back as society adjusts itself to the abuse. It was just such abuse of power by individuals in Government which resulted in Watergate. And the press cannot abuse its power without a similar result.

THE COMPUTER AND CIVIL LIBERTIES [5]

FRANCIS W. SARGENT [6]

In his State of the Union Message on January 30, 1974, President Richard M. Nixon argued that it is imperative "to define the nature and extent of the basic rights of privacy and to erect new safeguards to ensure those rights are respected." In making his plea he said:

> One measure of a truly free society is the vigor with which it protects the liberties of its individual citizens. As technology has advanced in America, it has increasingly encroached on one of those liberties, what I term the right of personal privacy. Modern information systems, data banks, credit records, mailing list abuses, electronic snooping, the collection of personal data for one purpose that may be used for another, all these have left millions of Americans deeply concerned about the privacy they cherish.

In response to the President's message the Department of Justice drafted a bill for the Senate (presented by Roman L. Hruska, Republican, Nebraska). An even more restrictive bill was introduced by the chairman of the Constitutional Rights subcommittee, Sam J. Ervin, Jr., of North Carolina (see *Congressional Record,* February 5, 1974). Senator Ervin argued:

> Yet if we have learned anything in this last year of Watergate, it is that there must be limits upon what the government can know about each of its citizens. Each time we give up a bit of information about ourselves to the government, we give up some of our freedom. For the more the government or any institution knows about us, the more power it has over us. When the government knows all of our secrets, we stand naked before official power. Stripped of our privacy, we lose our rights and privileges. The Bill of Rights then becomes just so many words.

[5] Delivered under the sponsorship of the Center for Criminal Justice, at the Student Union Building, Boston University, October 4, 1973. Quoted by permission.

[6] For biographical note, see Appendix.

Governor Francis W. Sargent of Massachusetts gave another view of the problem when he addressed a gathering at the Boston University Student Union Building Conference Auditorium, October 4, 1973. The meeting was sponsored by the Center for Criminal Justice at Boston University.

Governor Sargent expresses his thoughts in short, simple sentences, many under ten words in length. His direct style emphasizes his eagerness to reach his listeners.

I think we can all agree that in the last two decades a new force has swept across our society till today it dominates every phase of our lives.

I speak, of course, of the computer.

The effects of this new technology reach everywhere . . . into business . . . into industry . . . and most importantly into government.

Now let me be clear on one thing. I do not oppose this new technology by itself. What I do fear is the computer run wild . . . a technology which instead of serving, ends up controlling.

And further, I fear the new ethic which has arrived with the computer. Technical efficiency now reigns supreme in our society. The greatest value for the dollar.

Yet efficiency cannot be our only goal. We must also seek to protect individual liberties and rights . . . we must continue to deal with citizens as individuals, not as numbers on a card.

Some may say that the danger is hypothetical . . . that the computer presents little, if any, threat to the right of a citizen to be considered and treated as an individual.

Well, as the governor of this state, I can assure you that such confidence is misplaced. For we in Massachusetts have felt the edge of technology's sword . . . we know what it's like to try to curb the computer . . . and we have seen the depersonalization that so easily can occur.

For the last few months, Massachusetts has been battling the Federal Government to limit the extent to which the computer invades the privacy of our citizens. Specifically, this state has refused to join a national system for the collection and dissemination of personal criminal records.

Administered by the FBI, this National Crime Information Center is designed to include the criminal history systems of each state.

The Massachusetts system has been ready for some time. Yet we have refused to link up with the Federal NCIC.

We have taken this position because it has become clear that although we have established important safeguards on our criminal history system, the FBI has left its own system virtually uncontrolled.

We have said that only convictions would be recorded. But the Federal system also includes arrests *not* followed by conviction.

We have said that access would be limited essentially to law enforcement agencies. But the Federal system allows much wider access. Agencies not connected to law enforcement—even private credit companies—are permitted to see and use these confidential records.

We have established an independent watchdog committee to protect the privacy of the individual. But the Federal Government has no similar body.

And *we* have given the individual the right to see his file and correct it if it is wrong. But the Federal Government permits no such privilege. In fact, they have not even developed the means.

When the vast deficiencies of the Federal system became clear, this state had only one legitimate option.

The moment we joined the national system, our information would flow into their data bank and our safeguards would be rendered meaningless.

Therefore, on June 13th, I refused to allow Massachusetts to join with the Federal system.

And the sword fell.

The Justice Department brought suit against us in Federal court to force our hand.

Washington threatened to freeze $30 million in Small Business Administration loans if we did not yield.

The Defense Department announced that they would hold back 2,400 jobs unless it had access to our files.

Still I refused.

In fact, I joined a countersuit to force the Federal Government to establish safeguards similar to our own.

A week ago, Massachusetts emerged victorious from this confrontation. At that time, the Justice Department announced that it was dropping its suit against us.

And so for the moment the privacy of the citizens of this state is protected—at least when it concerns criminal records.

Unfortunately, however, the Federal Government has not limited its computer operations to criminal histories. It has also attempted to employ this new technology in the battle against drug abuse.

In 1972, the Federal Government set about to create a national information system to gather data on drug abuse. It came to be known as CODAP.

Theoretically, the idea of CODAP was and is sound. For better information is vital for the effective management, research and evaluation of programs.

In practice, however, the Government failed to create the necessary safeguards. It asked each drug treatment facility to provide identifying information on each person receiving treatment for drug problems . . . information to be fed into the CODAP computers.

The patient's name was not requested. Rather an identity code was devised that included the patient's sex, race, date of birth, zip code, and the first two letters of his mother's maiden and surname.

We were told that through this code, the patient's confidentiality could be protected.

On the surface this sounded excellent. But then Massachusetts investigated, and we quickly learned that when CODAP records are combined with other computer records, identities are very quickly discovered.

In fact, we found that the CODAP code was actually more exact than an individual's name. In a given geographical area, for example, individual clients could be determined with up to 98 percent accuracy.

So once again, I refused to let this state join a national information system.

As with NCIC, the Federal Government has backed down in CODAP. Massachusetts can continue to receive Federal funds, even though we will not deliver the requested information.

These then are the two major battles that we have fought to protect the individual . . . to curb the advance of the computer and of its ethic: efficiency over everything else.

But though we have won two significant victories, the basic dangers remain. If we are to meet them, we must learn the lessons of NCIC and of CODAP.

To begin with, we must understand that NCICs and CODAPs occur because too often public officials overlook the social implications of their programs.

Too often they are blinded by technical advancements . . . new designs . . . greater capabilities. Too often officials lose sight of the true purpose of social technology . . . aid to the individual.

We must understand that we do not protect the public safety by depriving individuals of their rights as citizens.

And we do not help a drug abuser by branding him for life . . . by undermining his faith in our treatment facilities.

Yet that is what NCIC threatens . . . that is what CODAP threatens. These programs are still two more examples of how the technology of computers can change the very meaning of man as an individual.

NCICs and CODAPs can let us consider a person—not as a unique individual with potentials for good and evil—but as the sum total of printouts supplied by interlocking personal data banks.

This is efficiency with all it can mean. Machine over man . . . system over individual.

Let us be clear though, the computer itself is not the danger . . . it is the ethic of the computer . . . the idea that man can be dealt with in the aggregate . . . that there are only groups out there . . . not individuals, men and women who need society's help.

The computer itself cannot do damage. But it leads too easily to dehumanized solutions to social problems.

Consider for example the new approaches we are witnessing in several states to deal with drug abuse . . . programs that consider the abuser not as one who needs help but as one who is a public enemy . . . one who is to be labeled and then forgotten.

However, drug abusers cannot be wished away. They must be dealt with one way or the other. If we choose to ignore their individuality . . . if we choose to toss them into the criminal justice system, we will not solve the problem.

In fact, all we will do is overburden our criminal justice system.

The dehumanized approach, the efficient approach cannot work. The regressive legislation we have seen in several states can only compound the problem.

Recent experience has shown that pushers are not becoming less common, they are only becoming more careful. In one state, for example, arrests have actually fallen 75 percent. Additionally, because of this regressive approach, the police are facing increased dangers when making an arrest. The reason is clear. A drug offender will not hesitate to shoot an officer if he has already earned mandatory life imprisonment for the abuse alone.

Further, the courts, already backlogged, will soon become truly jammed. Flexibility in the handling of cases will end as all defendants demand long, expensive jury trials.

And finally, our prisons will overflow with inmates having little at stake in maintaining order. Attica will be endlessly multiplied.

Such is and will always be the result of a dehumanized approach to the drug abuse problem. Such is the inevitable result of an ethic that ranks efficiency over the individuality of man.

These then are my concerns. We embark upon a dangerous course when we rush headlong into programs like NCIC or CODAP which threaten to undermine the rights and privacy of the individual.

Once we allow ourselves, for whatever reasons, to look beyond the individual as the measure of our social programs, we risk the development of so-called solutions . . . solutions which can only corrupt our society.

This is the real challenge we face as we attempt to use technology to solve our social problems. We can no longer abdicate our responsibilities. We can no longer let our desire for efficiency so overwhelm us that we forget that the goal of technology is to help man, not to enslave him.

In Massachusetts, we have discovered that the danger is not imaginary . . . but that it is real. And we have discovered how difficult it is to do battle against it.

It is a knowledge not limited to those in government. The citizens, too, realize the threat.

I'd like to read a letter I received from one frightened citizen.

> A scary thing happened to me last spring.
>
> A relative of mine got a job as a deputy sheriff. One bored night on dispatcher duty, he ran his entire family through the National Crime Information Center. Ten out of eleven of us were listed.
>
> His mother was listed because when she was eighteen, neighbors complained of a noisy sorority party. (No arrests.)
>
> His stepfather, a respected businessman, was listed because he complained to the police that he had *received* a bad check.
>
> Ten out of eleven of us! No criminal record. But we are on the files of the NCIC!
>
> P.S., I'll probably be listed again for writing this letter.

This is the danger we must confront. It is a danger we cannot afford to overlook.

RESTORING THE TIDEMARKS OF TRUST [7]

MALCOLM C. MOOS [8]

On May 20, 1973, Malcom C. Moos delivered the annual spring commencement address at Notre Dame University before an audience of more than twelve thousand graduates, parents, and friends in the university's Athletics and Convocation Center.

Moos knew that his listeners were chiefly interested in hearing his reactions to the unfolding Watergate scandal in Washington. "The presidency," he declared, "appears to be less visible and less available, shielded from public contact by layers and layers of bureaucracy until the cocoon is no longer transparent." Later in his speech, he made his most startling and dramatic statement: "The sum of allegations is that we were the victims of a coup d'état or an attempted coup." Yet many of those present probably did not realize the significance of this statement or appreciate his insight—at least not until the revelations of the Senate Watergate Committee's hearings began to make headlines the world over.

Malcolm Moos has had a full life in academia and politics. A former professor of political science at Johns Hopkins University, he has served as an adviser and speechwriter for President Dwight D. Eisenhower and former Governors Nelson Rockefeller of New York and William W. Scranton of Pennsylvania. In addition, he is a former president of the University of Minnesota, a noted author of several books on politics, and currently president of the Center for the Study of Democratic Institutions, in Santa Barbara, California.

Commencement speeches are often dull because they are abstract and full of platitudes, but that was not the case with the speech at Notre Dame. With his considerable experience as a speechwriter, Moos knew how to enliven his presentation through the inclusion of specific and personal references. In this one speech, he cited or quoted at least ten different persons, including Presidents Eisenhower and Kennedy; Senator Joseph McCarthy; the Italian journalist Oriana Fallaci; the Spanish philosopher Unamuno; and his old mentor from the Baltimore *Sun,* H. L. Mencken. Reflecting wit and good humor, he quoted *The Joy of*

[7] Delivered at the spring commencement ceremonies at Notre Dame University, South Bend, Indiana, May 20, 1973. Quoted by permission.

[8] For biographical note, see Appendix.

Cooking, used track-and-field meets as an analogy, alluded to himself as a "Minnesota Moos" and an "aging Moos," and inserted in his conclusion a delightful story about his encounter with an English reporter at a cricket match in Pakistan. These materials amplified his message and kept his speech brisk.

In making a direct application to his immediate audience, he suggested that the educators of the country must share the responsibility for Watergate, charging that they had taught their students "the price of everything and the value of nothing." He called upon the university to exert a positive influence for morality and urged his listeners to "reincarnate a commitment to democratic ideals and processes."

On January 18, 1961, promptly at 10:29 A.M. Sterling Green of the Associated Press said: "Thank you, Mr. President," and instantly, amidst a standing ovation from 309 journalists, Dwight David Eisenhower, thirty-fourth President of the United States, waved goodbye as he concluded his one hundred ninety-third news conference—his last.

Just the evening before, President Eisenhower had delivered a nationwide farewell broadcast. In it he spoke of "the conjunction of an immense military establishment and a large arms industry," which he pointed out wisely, was new in the American experience. "The total influence," he said, "economic, political, and even spiritual is felt in every city, every statehouse, every office of the Federal Government." And then he admonished the nation solemnly:

> In the councils of Government, we must guard against the acquisition of unwarranted influence, whether sought or unsought, by the military-industrial complex. . . . We must never let the weight of this combination endanger our liberties or democratic processes. We should take nothing for granted. Only an alert and knowledgeable citizenry can compel the proper meshing of the huge industrial and military machinery of defense with our peaceful methods and goals so that security and liberty may prosper together.

Although within three months Mr. Eisenhower's farewell address began attracting national and international scrutiny, only one reporter, Mr. William McGaffin of the Chicago *Daily News,* referred to it at the last news conference. "Mr. President," he queried, "you sounded a warning last night of the dangers to our democratic processes implicit in unparalleled military establishment. But some of your critics contend that liberty, the people's right to know, has suffered under your Administration because you have tolerated abuse of executive privilege in the Defense Department and other departments and agencies and because you did not hold frequent enough press conferences." To which Eisenhower responded briskly, "Well, they are critics and they have the right to criticize."

And so they do. And so the conflict between the need to know and the right not to tell in the highest councils of government has become the spectre that haunts every headline. Hanging over all of us like the deadliest of all mists is not disillusion, not despair, not disenchantment, not even distrust—but disbelief. Stated with the bark off of it, it has become difficult to believe in the existence of objective truth.

Some time ago a very wise and skilled journalist and a member of Parliament in England made the very cogent comment that "news is something somebody does not want you to print." He also went on to say that "the relation between the politician and newspapers are founded not on sympathy but antipathy. Both to some extent are rivals for influence over the public mind, and they take good care that neither should achieve a monopoly of it. It is here," Mr. Deeds insists altogether correctly, "where the great value of the relationship lies, because in countries where newspapers and politicians are in the same camp, freedom is threatened."

The theme that I will address myself to today is that of leadership and the need for visibility. I say visibility, although accountability is a much more fashionable word. But I would be the first to insist that accountability is really what is uppermost in our thoughts when we think critically about life at the top.

First, as a Minnesota Moos who has been chief executive

of a major state university for five years, let me say a word about my brief tenure. I say brief because Father Hesburgh, with twenty-one years, is the dean of us all. In the shapeless athenaeum of modern university life, the president is continually pounded and pelted by a blizzard of mind-clogging crises and problems: the recruitment and retention of the most adventurous faculty, students, and staff; the development of the most sensitive radar scopes to scout new, untried, nontraditional ideas; and the incredibly intricate task of orchestrating resources and personnel more efficiently in a more constricted budgetary environment. Finally, of course, he must not only continue to perform an expanding bundle of symbolic duties, but he must also react speedily to increased demands for accountability to his multiplying constituencies, and he must be responsive to the explosive elements of social scope that crisscross the nation.

Now, there are similarities between the presidency of a major university and the presidency of the United States. Both seem to have become a national lightning rod for varieties of public disaffection, distrust, and downright hostility. In the life of higher learning, the life of the mind, the presidency has entered an era of responsible reporting and instantly so. We presidents have learned, sometimes at great expense, that to maintain the public trust, we must be constantly visible, open, and forthright about our activities. In like manner, it would seem, the American presidency will enter the same era, also having learned at painful expense.

Over the years we have hesitated to tinker with the presidential system, in the halls of learning as well as the statehouse. And wisely so, for it has served us well as we have moved, crisis by crisis. But without tampering with structure, the times demand adventurous adaptation to the challenges of the hour. It is curious that while there is a movement toward openness at all other governmental levels and in higher education, that we hear so much of "executive privilege" and that the executive branch appears to be moving toward increasing levels of secrecy. It is also curious that during this same time of openness, the presidency appears to be less visible and less available, shielded from public contact by layers and layers of bureaucracy until the cocoon is no longer transparent.

Perhaps one of the most striking similarities between the president of a major university and the President of the United States is best summed up by Oriana Fallaci's pithy comment in her book, *If the Sun Dies:* "When it really sets out to, America can out-bureaucratize the best." Clearly, the bureaucratization of the presidency has had an insular impact on the relationship between the presidency and his constituents. But the exaltation and isolation of the presidency from the American people is a long story. It is a matter of power beyond what was contemplated—a staff system with inevitable justification—but so often the product of what Mr. Eisenhower used to complain of as "overzealous staff work," and finally, a remoteness beyond what was contemplated—almost a semicelestial presidency.

It is proper, for example, for the President to speak to the American people and use them as a megaphone to react upon the Congress, but I believe that the time has come in the confluence of events when the Chief Executive should speak to the Congress openly and regularly. President Kennedy, had he appeared before Congress immediately after the Bay of Pigs, might have given the legislators an opportunity to assess and understand the dilemma he faced. Or Eisenhower, after the embarrassment of the U-2 overflight, might have appeared before Congress with the opportunity for a vote of confidence. Icy distance from the House and Senate can only magnify the heated adversarial roles that the legislative and executive branches have begun to assume toward each other. Presidents of institutions of higher learning can attest to the need for continuous communication with their own "Congresses," the faculty-student senates. Those who have not maintained internal accord have found themselves in an isolation not of their own making.

The continuity of the American presidency, of course, continues on a term basis with periodic referendums for rejection or renewal. But the time has come to institutionalize a means of restoring the tidemarks of trust between the Executive and the Congress. In essence, I suggest the functional equivalent of a vote of confidence for having the President continuously accountable to the legislative branch.

We are reliving a period quite like that of the 1950s which brought a new term into the dictionary known as McCarthyism. At every conceivable gathering—dinner or cocktail party—people matched atrocity stories and there was a great wringing of hands about the dreadful state of affairs that was smothering the nation. But few did anything about it.

Today all eyes are trained on the exposé of abuses astride life at the top of our Government. As the McCarthy period taught us, there is no time when charges should be loosely made. Consequently, I hasten to point out . . . convictions already obtained and acts already admitted to support the statement I have just made. As though that were not bad enough, the allegations which are yet to be examined in congressional inquiries and in the courts are striking in their enormity. It must be faced that the sum of all the allegations is that we were the victims of a coup d'état or an attempted coup. I weigh my words carefully. I am aware that the strict definition of a coup d'état is "a sudden decisive exercise of force whereby the existing government is subverted." But, surely, an attempt to capture or retain control of a government by *illegal means* is action of the same genre.

Many of the principal "figures" involved are products of the silent generation following World War II. These are not men unschooled; almost all are products of higher education. This should give us at the universities particular reason to wonder what went wrong and why. Did we either through acts of commission or omission contribute in any way to the malaise which besets us?

Now academia has always been engaged in a search for truth. But have we passed that heritage on to our students? Is that an article of faith that has been rejected?

Yet the concern now is less with reality and more with appearance—the difference between what is and what appears to be. Can it be that "appearances" of the sort projected by television have had a greater impact than the "reality" we contend we deal with in higher education? Have we taught men the price of everything and the value of nothing? Did higher education merely provide tools and technology, but no sense of ethics and morality to temper the far-flung influence of the military-industrial complex, an awesome floating power largely free of restraint?

In both the era of the silent generation of the fifties and the youthquake of the sixties, we have witnessed a lack of commitment to democratic ideals and processes. And we permitted situations to develop where we did not respect the rights of others. Regrettably, at some of our finest tradition-laden temples of freedom, the right to listen as well as to speak was flagrantly violated and some of those scars have not only been altogether erased, but they helped speed the university's swift fall from grace in the public esteem.

Is it unfair, then, to suggest that the happenings at our universities contributed to create a climate which permitted men at the pinnacle of political power to see nothing morally wrong in dealing cavalierly with democratic ideals, processes, and justice? I ask you to ponder that question, not as an exercise of self-flagellation but as a way of pointing up what needs to be done. For whatever the universities' responsibility, or lack of it, they can play a major role in restoring the tidemarks of trust.

Over the years there have been many disparaging themes about dethroning the eggheads from positions of influence in public affairs. What we need is just the opposite. Let us enthrone the egghead who is worthy of trust and the institutions that have nurtured their growth and immense capabilities. My source and documentation for this article of faith is unimpeachable—an authoritative volume titled *The Joy of Cooking*. Boldly and in immeasurably clear language it sets forth this principle: "Treat eggs gently. They like this consideration and will respond to kindness." Again from an equally authoritative source another stern warning: "The first principle that cannot be impressed too strongly is that eggs cook with a very low degree of heat."

Our universities comprise the nation's most inventive spearheads. They have been through a traumatic ordeal—some of it deservedly. But we need to restore our faith and reaffirm our confidence in them. This happens to be the track season. Remember, universities do not excel at the 100-yard dash. They are not sprinters. They are not geared to perform over the short course. They are distance runners and their performance and quest for excellence is enriched and ennobled over the long stretch.

In preparing this presentation, I did so under the heavy and constant reminder that I was born during a war and that for twenty-four of my fifty-six years—almost half of my life—this nation has been at war. And we are still not clear of conflict that defies the intellect. Not only the war, but the constellation of social, economic, and now environmental issues have brought colleges and universities to the very brink of perhaps their most difficult ordeal and trial.

During the first third of this century, as Spain gasped and choked with internal disorders and descended toward total collapse under governments unable to govern, the brilliant philosopher, Unamuno, wanted to make all of Spain his classroom. He desired not just a chair as a platform at Salamanca, but really as a pulpit to give him an eminence to educate all of Spain. The Spanish government had insisted and indeed promulgated the doctrine that politics and teaching were incompatible. But Unamuno countered otherwise. He declared that politics and teaching were the same thing. In essence, he argued that while politics is teaching on a national level, teaching is politics on a personal level. And when his critics denounced him for speaking in paradoxes, his rejoinder was that paradoxes could not be disposed of when it was necessary to arouse and awaken an indolent nation—to rattle its very spine to the necessity of responding to challenge.

Clearly, members of university communities—faculty, students, and civil service personnel alike—wish to be heard on their deep-felt concerns for the way the nation is headed —and lustily so. But the axis of university life is not one of taking corporate positions. Ideally a university is like a live and open microphone where all the expressions and ideas of its component parts can be picked up and their vibrations stir response and enlighten debate across the nation.

The activism that seeks to convert universities, as institutions, into political partisans, thumping for this or that ideological position, is a threat to the unique relationship between the university and external social and political institutions. Specifically, universities are uniquely the place where society builds its capacity to gather, organize and transmit knowledge; to analyze and clarify controverted issues; and to define alternative responses to issues. Ideology is properly an object of study or scholarship. But when it becomes the starting point of intellect, it threatens the function uniquely cherished by institutions of learning.

Like the individual scholar, the university itself is no longer the dispassionate seeker after truth once it adopts controverted causes which go beyond the duties of scholarship, teaching, and learning. But unlike the individual scholar, the university has no colleague to light the fires of debate on controverted public issues. And unlike the individual scholar, it cannot assert simply a personal choice of judgment when it enters the field of political partisanship, but must seem to assert a corporate judgment which obligates, or impinges upon, or towers over what might be contrary choices by individuals within its community. To this extent, it loses its unique identity among our social institutions. And to this extent, it diminishes its capacity to protect the climate of freedom which nourished the efficiency of freedom. The activists who want most passionately freedom of individual choice and freedom for commitment to causes should understand that, when they seek to commit the university to their chosen political cause, they threaten the unique capacity of the university to walk the razor's edge of being both in and out of the world, and yet simultaneously in a unique relationship with it.

It is very easy for those of us who seek the eye of the hurricane to ride out the storm to become immensely irritated at how the press and the media handle news. How often those of us in university life have been belted by well-meaning, dedicated alumni who have chided us during the past six difficult years for not showing the good side of university life. Why, they insist, have the tiny willful minorities dominated the television screen or the front pages?

The press, of course, have come under a drumfire of criticism for seeming to give unbalanced coverage. But the universities reflect the strain and stress of society in microcosm. Willful minorities, moreover, have a way of jagging history.

It was the willful minority, the Bolsheviks, that overturned the majority, the Mensheviks, in the Russian Revolution, for which a terrible price has been paid. One might well ask, glancing back over our shoulders, what might have been the result in the tides of modern Russian history if the country had had a free press.

Now, our antiquarian tradition of commencement exercises ordains that appropriately some word of advice and counsel be transmitted by the speaker to the graduating class. I have carefully refrained from so doing. I would remind you, though, that no age has a monopoly on madness and even a madcap movement confronted by a repressive force is like a kite against the wind. The stronger the wind the higher the kite flies.

We are confronted at times by an astounding velocity of change. When I was a boy, Miss America stood five feet one. Today she stands five feet nine. I will not comment on her other measurements, but all about us we are reminded that our problems are more explosively stacked.

And they do not sink out of sight. As my old mentor, the demolition expert on the Baltimore *Sun,* once spoke of the "vacuum President: His way of dealing with the problems confronting him is to avoid them, as a sensible man avoids an insurance solicitor or his wife's relatives." Nor is a long gone French prime minister correct when he said, "The art of politics lies not in dealing with fundamental problems, but in keeping quiet those who raise them."

No, the late great artist Picasso found the touchstone when during a life that stretched over ninety years, he often referred to the privilege of the artist which is "to do," and when critics asked him what he was trying to explain or convey—what he was trying to get at—his rejoinder was, "You mustn't talk to the driver."

I have a fierce faith that your generation will invoke the privilege of the artist to do, and vigorously so, whether it be somewhere in the rainbow of the arts and humanities, medicine—biomedical or spare-parts surgery—science, that of the solitary tinkerer and investigator, or in the drafty rooms of politics. So be free. Feel loose in your harnesses and do not be dismayed or deterred by the critics haranguing the driver from the back seat or from sheltered burrows.

Let us reincarnate a commitment to democratic ideals and processes. Because America that has been so adventurous, so creative and so boldly buccaneerish in the building of industry, science, commerce, finance, and a dazzling technology—the envy of mankind, let us not drift downward spiritually with only a cosmetic concern for the light of the mind that tells us what is right.

So, as an aging Moos, let me conclude with the story of my first experience with a cricket match in Pakistan. Completely baffled after the first twenty minutes, I turned to an English newsman and asked: "What is the object of this game?" In a manner most condescending to one I am certain he regarded as a peasant from the prairie provinces, he stared at me stonily and said: "The object—the object, my dear sir, is to get on with it!"

So saying, Notre Dame graduating class of 1973, we should be about our work.

RAISING THE FALLEN IMAGE OF BUSINESS [9]

STANLEY J. GOODMAN [10]

"The appalling drop in the reputation of business in our lifetime is a fact and it is disturbing and dangerous," asserted Stanley J. Goodman, chairman of the May Department Stores Company, of St. Louis, Missouri, on January 7, 1974. This frank admission probably startled the eight hundred top management representatives from department and specialty stores from throughout the United States and abroad who were assembled at the annual luncheon of the Association of Buying Offices, held in New York City's Hilton Hotel during the annual convention of the National Retail Merchants Association [NRMA].

Mr. Goodman was responding to the growing evidence that business and industry, like education, government, and religion, are suffering a decline in prestige—hurt, no doubt, by the revelation of the illegal contributions made by large corporations to the fund for the reelection of President Nixon. This and the success of consumer groups under the leadership of Ralph Nader and others reinforces the conclusion of Professor Irving Kristol of New York University who argues that "the American corporation is in serious trouble. . . . It is true that the corporate image is in a worse condition than it deserves. But it is also true that this image is not going to be changed by the minor magic of 'public relations.' There is no reason why Operation Candor should be restricted to the White House" (*National Observer,* January 26, 1974).

The audience, accustomed to hearing calls for better advertising and slicker promotional and public relation strategies, apparently reacted favorably to this frank appraisal. Said Goodman: "Nothing I've said or written in forty years has brought me such response" (New York *Times,* February 19, 1974).

The speech is an excellent one for many reasons. First, it clearly follows a problem-solution formula, with numerous signposts included to assist the listener in following its development. Second, the speech is filled with specific details and evidence. Third, the language is simple, direct, and meaningful.

[9] Delivered at the annual luncheon of the Association of Buying Offices, Hilton Hotel, New York City, January 7, 1974. Quoted by permission.

[10] For biographical note, see Appendix.

And, fourth, the introduction and conclusion are highly appropriate in forwarding the speaker's goals. In theme, as well as in structure, the speech is noteworthy; indeed, it is refreshing to find a speaker who tells his listeners what they need to be told instead of what they want to be told.

When I was a boy someone gave me a Horatio Alger novel. I read it with a fast-beating heart. The virtuous rise of my penniless hero in a distinguished business was thrilling, inspiring, so *right*.

How the picture has changed! A Louis Harris survey that has been measuring public confidence in business over the past five years reveals a massive loss of faith in business in that period. Where 58 percent of the people expressed confidence in major companies five years ago, it has now fallen to 29 percent, just half. It is even worse with young people. Only 15 percent, 1 in 7, of the eighteen-to-twenty-year-olds expressed confidence in the way business is run.

Here is another picture, even more shattering to our egos. In a recent Harvard survey they asked a broad sampling of children of various ages this question, "Do you think men who run large companies are honest?" When they got to the age of eleven and older, more than half of the kids answered, "No." We are still solid with the infants, for the moment.

This appalling drop in the reputation of business in our lifetime is a fact and it is disturbing and dangerous.

What went wrong? How has it happened that American business management, the darling of the free world economy, extolled by a best-selling French book only a few years ago as a unique force that was changing the world, should now find itself in the doghouse at home?

Of course we have company. The public has also lost confidence, according to the same Louis Harris survey, in the Federal Government (this was before Watergate), in the military, and in organized religion, although not as dramatically as the loss of confidence in business.

What is wrong with the public's relationship to business is more than the rejection of the Establishment. There is a growing questioning of the aims of business which I believe is spreading in the free world. Two years ago I gave a series of lectures on management at a European seminar attended by about fifty young European men and women from business, education, and government, including a number from Communist-bloc countries. They all had a lively interest in management techniques, but I was somewhat taken aback at their prevalent skepticism about management motives. When I stated that a company's management was working for the stockholders and that its long-range objective was growth, the word "growth" unleashed quite a storm in the classroom. The fact that the right kind of growth is clearly necessary to support continued life on this planet did not stop them from an automatically negative emotional response to the very idea of growth. Incidentally the storm did not come from the Communist-bloc people; they just sat there perhaps amused at the current capitalist state of mind.

This distrust of growth is just as prevalent here. The Gross National Product is the most widely-used general yardstick for how the economy is doing, and GNP is now being compiled by most of the countries in the free world. Well, GNP-fixation is increasingly under attack, and what the growing chorus of voices is saying is that the quantity of goods and services produced is no longer acceptable as the measure of progress, that there is too much worship of quantity instead of quality in today's life.

But aside from all this, business has in many ways been its own worst enemy in the eyes of the American public. All the way back to the nineteenth century business has an almost unbroken record of opposing legislation that the public thinks is good. The Sherman Anti-Trust Act, the Federal Reserve Act, the Federal Trade Commission Act, the Securities Exchange Act—we fought every one of them and lost. The Child Labor Act, the Fair Labor Standards Act, the Old Age and Survivors' Insurance Benefits Act, the Federal Housing acts, the Marshall Plan, the Federal Education Act, the Poverty Program, and Medicare—all the same story, business opposing, trying to hold the clock back and the legislation passing anyway.

Who is there among us today that feels all this legislation was bad for business? It has become the environment in which business as a whole has thrived and enjoyed unprecedented prosperity and vitality. The thoughtful businessman would agree, I think, that for the most part this pattern of legislation has updated our free enterprise system and made it viable under today's conditions, that it has been good for our society and good for business.

But unfortunately business leadership did not see it that way as it was happening, and so it behaved in a paradoxical way: forward-looking in running its own business, the opposite in considering social needs and problems. And unfortunately this image of business as the bad guy who is against good things is now intensified by the great national trauma of Watergate, and I shudder to think what a public opinion survey taken now would score on business motives and integrity.

Now, on top of all this, the energy crisis raises doubts as to how good business is in planning its own sphere. The man in the street, worried about heat, running his car, getting on an airplane, and maybe losing his job through the long reach of the oil shortage, is not giving high marks to our petroleum industry for its role in the drama. Nor is he full of admiration for the foresight of our great automobile industry in providing cars that measure up to today's needs.

This collapse of the public regard for business is not something we can take lightly. If the public generally feels that the aims of business are at cross purposes with those of the people of our country, if a majority believes that businessmen are apt to be dishonest, making money by deception or conspiracy, then we are in bad shape indeed.

Then for the first time in generations, our economy, for all its vaunted efficiency, may find itself in conflict with the people it serves, and the root purpose of the free enterprise system could come under serious question.

What would the future prospects of the free enterprise system be if the elected government which has to be responsive to the people came more and more into open warfare with a business community that is not responsive to the people. Government understanding of business would be nonexistent. The very functioning of business organizations would be undermined by the poisons of bad internal morale and vanishing pride in the job. And the future of the world-famous American management prowess would be stunted by repelling the best young brains and talent.

In other words, the fallen image of business is not just an unpleasant fact. It is dangerous. And business should feel some urgency and some anxiety about it. If you had someone running a part of your business who had lost the confidence and respect of the people he is supposed to serve, and who has taken a losing position time after time on important issues, what would you do? If the public is convinced that the things that have to do with the quality of life are being hurt not helped by business, then we are on a collision course and Horatio Alger should be spinning in his grave.

I am making this point to you as retailers because in the whole American economy there is no industry as close to the consumer as ours is, or as schooled in studying the life of the people, their likes and dislikes and their aspirations. How can we forget that the customer who is "always right" in the retailer's creed is also the public who thinks business is nearly always wrong? You can't face these facts and not want to do something to win back the confidence of the American people.

And don't delude yourself that the public likes retailers any better than the rest of business. In the Harris survey on the confidence question, retail stores scored one percentage point lower than major companies in general. We are in the same boat with the rest of the economy, but we should be more aware of what the weather is. And I hope we are. After all, what did the NRMA take as a theme for the convention that opens today? "Look Out! Here Comes Tomorrow!" Retailing as an industry and we as retailers, I believe, have an important opportunity open to us to look out on tomorrow and show the way for other industries in developing the kind of social responsiveness that can win back public confidence and put business where it belongs in the mainstream of American aspirations.

Whether or not we will come to live with a social audit whereby corporations will assess their social performance in as systematic a manner as they now assess their financial performance is not of pressing importance. Let's get the performance and the measurement will take care of itself. These are the main elements in that performance:

1. The Consumer

As long as we have a free market economy, the consumer is in the driver's seat. And since the sovereign consumer is also the voter, an elected government must be active in defense of the consumer. Hence the Food & Drug Administration, the Federal Trade Commission, the Office of Consumer Affairs, and the other government bodies dedicated to consumerism. None of these would win a popularity contest with business managements.

How smart are we to pass off consumerism as an irritating nuisance? I don't know anybody in retailing who is building his business by cheating his customers. The customer is free to take his business wherever he wants. He is not stupid, and he will stay away from the retailer who tries to get a hold of his dollar by deception or who sells him substandard merchandise and falls down on service. It should follow then that consumerism, the growing awareness by the consumer of his rights and the demand for higher standards of performance, is surely an opportunity and not a threat for retailing. The public is out there judging us as consumers, and therefore we should in a sense put the consumer on the organization chart of our business. Isn't it good business to do this? Instead of hoping we get by with something less?

What we need, it seems to me, is a systems approach to this all-important problem, namely to anticipate what the customer wants to know before, during, and after purchase, what the customer has a right to expect in the performance of the article we sell and in the event of a malfunction. As the head of your business you may think that this is what is being done, and yet how your middle management handles it may be something else again. Their eyes are on the cash register and unless they are thoroughly indoctrinated from the top down, opportunism will creep in. Whenever I see a customer sign in one of our stores beginning, "For Your Convenience," I wonder if the customer really finds whatever it is we are doing more convenient for her or for us.

The standards of inspection applied by manufacturers to the products we sell are getting lower and lower and it does not help consumer confidence to read about the hundreds of thousands of automobiles recalled for defects not detected before delivery. It seems to me that retailing has a duty and an opportunity both to the consumer and the manufacturer to police quality standards and screen out merchandise with a high incidence of customer disappointment.

Advertising of course is one of the major battlefields of consumerism. We are in the age of accountability for advertising, and why shouldn't we be? The temptations to make a fast buck in sales promotion are strong, but we have all known businesses that have been destroyed by the wrong kind of promotion practices. Advertising is our major means of communicating with our customers and we underestimate their intelligence at our peril. Just as we have internal auditors to make sure that our accounting practices will get high marks from the outside auditors, so we need to subject our own advertising to internal tests before release for publication. And these tests should be stringent: not just the avoidance of falsification or deception, but making sure that the message in the ad cannot be misunderstood to the customer's disadvantage. Too few advertisers realize the power of candor in communicating with their customers. And some of the most productive "new wave" advertising uses candor as a selling strategy.

And so I say that in spite of all the headaches they may have caused, government standards in advertising have been a good thing for business in that they have helped to raise advertising credibility at a time when other kinds of credibility are falling. There are signs of continuing progress. The children's industry has made a real improvement in shaping advertising constructively from the consumer's point of view. Three industries—major appliances, furniture, and automobiles—have set up consumer action panels, which maintain liaison between the companies and government consumer agencies with promising potential as an approach to the problem.

2. *The Environment*

Business ultimately has as big a stake in saving our environment as the rest of the nation. A company that pollutes its environment is going to find it increasingly difficult to attract bright young people to its work force. If America ruins its natural beauty and destroys the health of its citizens, it will be a less prosperous country and a poorer market for the products of business. The difficulty is that saving the environment involves exceedingly complex interacting forces, such as we are now seeing to our dismay, in the collision of the gasoline shortage with automobile pollution standards. What is clear is that if we leave government alone to cope with these frustratingly difficult problems, we could get solutions that produce bigger evils than the ones they cure. Only with the best brains in business working with the government can we hope to find the right way.

3. Minorities

A discouragingly difficult area in which some industries are still very backward. The retailing industry is probably one of the bright spots in minority hiring, but there is undoubtedly room for further improvement. Have we done enough with stores in minority areas, and with the management staffing of those stores as well as special attention to their merchandise assortments? Have we any impediments in the way of doing enough business with minority suppliers? Are we as an industry alive to the opportunities that could be opened by a fuller encouragement of the creative talents of our minority citizens?

4. The Sexes

Improving job opportunities for women is overdue, perhaps another example of how the economic sphere lags behind the political sphere. The big coming bulge in the twenty-five to thirty-five young adult group of our population will be more than ever made up of working married women, and the supply of female talent for business will be an all-time high. A generation of girls who have done as well as the boys at school are not going to be content to do less well in business. There is therefore a tremendous opportunity ahead for us in building the role of women in the management of our business, whose customers are largely female and where women executives can therefore make a special contribution. Is there any other industry which comes within a mile of retailing in being right for upgrading the female participation in business? And interestingly enough, such a program would not only be socially desirable, it would in my opinion prove immediately profitable.

5. *The Community*

When it comes to community problems the record is clear that very little can be accomplished without business leadership. The difficulty is that the top management of large corporations in our country have travel schedules and job demands that leave a totally inadequate amount of time available for community activities. Perhaps better recognition of how destructive urban decay is to our national life and therefore to our corporations, would suggest some organizational restructuring of management to cope more effectively with the problem. As for health and welfare agencies and the arts, business is already doing a creditable job of support and getting very little public credit for it.

Let's agree then that tomorrow's manager must have more social objectives and achieve them in a measurable way. What would be the steps that need to be taken? Those who have given the most thought to these questions generally see three:

1. The chief executive officer of the company gets converted. That is the easiest step and there are many companies that would score low on a social audit whose chief executive is personally in tune with social objectives.
2. The next step is to get staff executives on a high level whose responsibilities are aimed at the social objectives. This sets up clearer definement of the goals to be achieved, the standards of measurement, and the information flow.
3. The final step is to get these goals into the objectives of the line operation so that they are recognized at the action level as being real and not just conversation. The line executive, living under constant pressure to produce bottom-line results, cannot be expected to be responsive to social goals without a good deal of work from topside in the organization. Ultimately what has to happen is that the social objec-

tive becomes just as real and everyday as the economic objective and as much a way of life all along the management trail.

This process is going to take time, and one cannot avoid some concern about whether there will be enough of a cure in time to save the patient.

But there are three things that business can do right now that would make a big difference. The first is finding a way to work with the government positively on the implementation of these social objectives. That would put business in a new posture, not fighting the trend but embracing it and then saying to the Administration: "You have a staggeringly difficult task ahead in tackling all of these social problems in America. With the best of intentions, you have had disillusion and frustration, such as in public housing and urban development, where the results have been disappointing and the money spent enormous. Planning and implementation are our business. We are concerned about our common social objectives and we want to help you achieve those objectives if you will let us."

There is a big selling job to be done because the government's understanding of how business operates is as low as their trust in our motives. But they must face up to the poor track record the Administration has had so far in a number of the social programs.

When the billion-dollar programs buy more frustration than solution, it is not for want of sincerity on the part of the legislators and administrators, but rather because of built-in disabilities in the follow-through. The government's main concern in staffing the offices charged with carrying out these programs seems to be to get people whose dedication to the aims of the program is the main requisite. As a result they are apt to wind up with a staff that is long on conceptual thinking, short on knowledge of how our complex economy works, and low on action skills. It is as if you put your research director in charge of the business.

Let's just look at one example, the Environmental Protection Association. Notwithstanding current energy complications, the general public was probably more unanimously in favor of trying to save our environment than any other program the Federal Government has attempted. And so what happened? A budget of $4.6 billion was assigned to the EPA, and ten thousand people were hired. A more dedicated band did not exist, and the troops began to march. Then one day the state of California wakes up to find that a state implementation plan was up for adoption which would so drastically have reduced motor vehicle traffic that the results would have been catastrophic for southern California's economy which depends so much on mobility. The point is that the administrators of the EPA are performing a difficult and complicated operation with little knowledge of the anatomy of the patient. If there had not been a last-minute public reaction resulting in a one-year delay, southern California might have had chaos along with the clean air. The objective was right, the implementation wrong.

Business has to do a selling job to convince the government that it can be trusted and that it will help get the job done and spare the Administration the embarrassment of well-meaning failures. A convincing point in this connection is the widespread development of long-range planning in American business in the past decade. The in-house skills that business has today for appraising future developments with professional competence and working with five- and ten-year plans updated each year, all of this should not only be a common ground for building a working relationship with government, but also should grow social responsiveness into the lifestyle of the corporation.

A good example of the right way for us to work with the government on these things is what has happened so far on energy conservation in the retail industry. The heads of NRMA and the American Retail Federation . . . said in effect: There are two ways to attack energy conservation in the retail industry. You can spell out in detail what every retailer must do and must not do to achieve optimum energy saving—that is the wrong way. Or you can tell us how much energy you want to save and have us take that on as an objective and put our best brains into achieving or surpassing your objective. The second way was agreed upon, and I hope we can stay with it and continue to do a much better job of energy conservation than many other industries.

Faced with what is sure to be a continuing flow of social problem legislation, if business will shed its negative stance and take a positive lead in the inevitable changes, it will accomplish these things: (1) condition its own middle managers to a recognition that social objectives are part of the customer-satisfying process; (2) improve the quality of the laws and their implementation; and (3) begin to persuade the public that business is a constructive force in our lives.

Another way to raise our image with the public is to raise our image with our own employees. Too often management takes it for granted that its employees hold the company in high regard. I am afraid that if a survey were made of employees along the same lines as the Louis Harris survey about public confidence in business, we would find much the same distressing picture. The employees of business are after all a major sector of the public, and we are deceiving ourselves if we think that our own employees love us while they go on having a low opinion of business in general.

What I am saying is that charity should begin at home, and if we want to be more responsive to the public we should begin by being more responsive to our own employees. If the 67 million Americans who are employed by business had a high opinion of their company managements, it would be impossible for only 29 percent of the public to have confidence in corporate leadership. This is telling us that job dissatisfaction must be widespread.

It seems to me, therefore, that we need to study employee attitudes, be concerned with how they feel about their jobs and whether their jobs are structured in a way that can give them job satisfaction.

This is not an easy one to cure, but the point needs to be made that an early step on the road to social responsiveness for business is to become more responsive to the employees' happiness, to devote more study to ways of job enrichment and job satisfaction for rank-and-file people as well as the bright young stars. Part of job enrichment would be better and more thoughtful structuring of the job itself and this may require some creative engineering. If McDonald can generate enthusiasm in young people for dishing out hamburgers, if Marriott Hotels can find a way to make waitresses and porters seem genuinely interested in the guests, and if United Parcel Service not only gets the package to you quickly but with a deliveryman who seems your friend, all these things point to what can and should be done on a high priority basis by American business if it is to begin to repair its damaged public image and insure its future role in American society.

Actions speak louder than words, but even if business makes real headway along these lines and can achieve visible real action in response to the social needs, there remains a big job to be done in educating the public about the business sector of our society. Few businessmen realize how wild are people's notions about business. In a survey in which people were asked how much after-tax profit business makes on the average, the responses were clustered around a figure of 28 percent! That in itself casts us in the role of the profiteering villain, and it says a lot about the poor job that we have done in communicating, not only to the public, but to our employees. With all of the communications skills in the sales promotion forces of business, surely we ought to be able to do a better job of getting rid of harmful fantasies in the public's mind. I am not saying that we can cure our image problem with propaganda, but at least we ought to be able to bring what people perceive about business a little closer to reality.

Business needs more positive visibility. It seems as if almost the only time the public hears from business is when it is being sold something, or when some business scandal is reported in the news. Retailing in particular has very low visibility as an industry. No doubt because retailers are so numerous and competitive they are not strongly perceived by the public as an industry in the same sense as are steel or oil or automobiles. Nor does the Washington Administration seem to give retailing the weight that it deserves considering its strategic closeness to the consuming and voting public. Therein lies a great challenge and opportunity for the NRMA in the years ahead.

Now let me summarize what I hope has not been too pious a message. We are meeting here today at a time of mounting concern about what faces all of us in the short range, when many of us have come here from some rather heavy meetings about spring plans and expense budgets. The NRMA has aptly reflected our state of mind in the slogan of this sixty-third annual convention, "Look Out! Here Comes Tomorrow!"

Now I am not considered a visionary. My boys at the May company would say I am a pretty tough results-oriented guy.

But my experience has taught me that top management should mentally live in the future. And that what we call bifocal management, focused both on the near and the far view, is the only way to make it in a fast-changing, problem-ridden world. Throughout the history of this planet, those living things that were not programmed to adapt to changing conditions became extinct. In the same way we have seen companies and industries rise and fall.

We need to listen to what Buckminster Fuller keeps saying: "Man was designed to be a success." So was the American free enterprise system. With all its faults, the world has seen nothing to compare with the creative release of human energy produced by the free market system manned by resourceful industrious people. Profits are what keep it all in motion, and if profits dwindle to a marginal level, the economy will wither into atrophy. And high profits for the most efficient should never be thought of as going counter to the social needs of our society, because it is precisely the companies who are good enough to achieve high profits in a competitive environment that will be good enough to get results on social problems. Don't expect much of a contribution to society from the business that is struggling for survival. And American business management has the energy and resourcefulness to do well for society without doing less well in their business.

There can be no doubt that people everywhere are weighed down with more and deeper concerns than this nation has had in a long time. But we must not let these concerns degenerate into fear and loss of self-confidence. Some of our troubles will turn to our benefit. The oil embargo will bring a faster solution to the energy problem which was there all along. Watergate should bring a raising of ethical standards throughout the fabric of our society for many years to come.

So we need to lift our eyes from the short-range problems that bedevil us and see the long-range concern of our people for the quality of life in addition to the quantity of goods.

I believe therefore that the American corporation has come to a moment of change, of fundamental rethinking of where it is going and what it is all about. As a nation we must integrate social and economic goals, and as business managers we must assume the responsibility to meld social and economic achievement, so that the national yardstick can evolve from Gross National Product to Gross Social Product and business be judged not just for the quantity but for the quality of profits.

Twenty years ago a Secretary of Defense received a good deal of flack for saying, "What's good for General Motors is good for the country." Now perhaps it is time to turn this around and say, "What's good for the people is good for business."

THE POLITICAL QUESTION OF AMNESTY

THEOLOGY AND AMNESTY [1]

ROBERT NEWTON BARGER [2]

"The acid of the Vietnam war still gnaws at the national psyche. . . . For amnesty seems to be the one issue that could stir up those deep and dormant passions about the war and raise questions which no one wants to face," said Kermit Lansner in *Newsweek* (April 8, 1974). But in the year elapsed since the close of the war the issue has changed from a "political unmentionable" to a topic of "active congressional scrutiny" (Guy Halverson, *Christian Science Monitor*). A Gallup poll of March 5, 1973, estimated that 78 percent of the persons interviewed would allow resisters to return to the United States either unconditionally or with certain requirements (just over a quarter approved "unconditional" amnesty and the remainder insisted on some kind of military or nonmilitary service, or fines). Of those interviewed, 10 percent insisted on jail sentences and 12 percent opposed return under any circumstances (*Congressional Record,* March 18).

In March 1974 the House Subcommittee on Courts, Civil Liberties and the Administration of Justice held a hearing on amnesty. Lieutenant General Leo E. Benade, the deputy assistant secretary of defense, opposed amnesty, arguing that it "would have a serious detrimental impact on morale and discipline of our armed forces." At the other extreme, Representative Bella S. Abzug (Democrat, New York) advocated unconditional amnesty for all classes of essentially nonviolent resisters, "including not only draft evaders and deserters but antiwar demonstrators." A proposal for conditional amnesty was presented by former Secretary of the Army Robert F. Froehlke, Senator Robert Taft, Jr. (Republican, Ohio), and Representative Edward I. Koch (Democrat, New York).

The three classes of resisters under consideration for amnesty were draft evaders, deserters, and those who received less than

[1] Speech delivered at the University Methodist Church, Peoria, Illinois, November 11, 1973. Previously included in *Amnesty: What Does It Really Mean?* published by the Committee for a Healing Repatriation. Copyright Robert Newton Barger 1974. Quoted by permission.

[2] For biographical note, see Appendix.

honorable discharges for one reason or another. Estimates of numbers in each category vary. Representative Abzug claimed that some 600,000 young Americans "are still prisoners of the war system." She estimated that 52,000 men resisted the draft, 7,000 of whom were classified as felons and 39,000 of whom awaited prosecution. She said that 32,000 men went AWOL after induction and were thus classified as deserters; 30,000 to 50,000 left the country; and some 450,000 received less than honorable discharges from the armed services (*Congressional Record,* March 14, 1974). Her figures, though, were larger than those later released by the Departments of Justice and Defense (New York *Times,* April 16, 1974) and presented to Congress by Representative Robert W. Kastenmeier (Democrat, Wisconsin). According to those statistics, only 9,167 men were actually convicted of draft-law violations; 4,000 were prosecuted for desertion; and 28,000 classified as deserters are still at large, with only 10 percent believed to be living outside the country.

The Rev. Robert Newton Barger of the University of Illinois Newman Foundation preached from a prepared text a sermon on amnesty at the University United Methodist Church, in Peoria, Illinois, on November 11, 1973. Dale A. Kooi explains: "Our Social Concerns Commission requested Father Barger to speak at our church as part of a several-week program informing our people about the issues involved in amnesty so that they might better express themselves with informed opinions." Father Barger was well prepared for this assignment and later assembled a publication on the subject entitled *Amnesty: What Does It Really Mean?* (published by the Committee for a Healing Repatriation). He also testified before the House subcommittee when it was holding its amnesty hearings.

The argumentation of the sermon is excellent. After offering three possible positions on the amnesty question, Father Barger chose the one that is the least extreme and that several factions could conceivably support. In developing his argument for leniency, he cited many scriptural passages to support his premises. After studying the sermon, Harold Mixon, an associate professor at Louisiana State University, pointed out: "Many sermons use Scripture primarily for illustrative purposes; however, the present sermon employs the Bible as a source of evidence in building logical proof and in that respect is rather unusual."

Today the United States of America, our homeland, is a nation divided, and as President Abraham Lincoln has reminded us, a house divided against itself cannot long stand. We have wounds, and they need to be healed. We are not at one, and so we stand in *urgent* need of reconciliation. The Vietnam war, whose decade-long duration was responsible for much of the division which we experience, has not left us totally at peace, even though it is now over. There is still the question before us: what to do with the war resisters. This question involves a *tension* between justice on the one hand, and mercy on the other. The resolution that we make of this tension between justice and mercy will provide the answer to what kind of reconciliation we can reasonably expect. In other words, how we treat those who have conscientiously evaded the draft or deserted from the war will determine in large part whether we will, or will not, have that domestic tranquillity of which our Constitution speaks.

I am going to make here some theological observations on the *political* question of amnesty. I would like to say at the outset that I am well aware of the danger of attempting to take concepts from the *spiritual* realm and apply them in the *political* order. The brilliant Protestant theologian, Reinhold Niebuhr, in his classic study entitled *Moral Man and Immoral Society,* has expressed a healthy pessimism about the possibility of making an individualistic ethic apply to a collective such as a nation-state. But even such a realist as Niebuhr goes on to say: "Every genuine passion for social justice will always contain a religious element within it. Religion will always leaven the idea of justice with the ideal of love. It will prevent the idea of justice, which is a politico-ethical ideal, from becoming a purely political one, with the ethical element washed out." So, theology can and must supply ideals for the reflection of the national sovereign . . . and in the case of a democracy such as ours, the sovereign is *us.* The government is responsible to us, and that is why, ultimately, we the people, will get the kind of justice or mercy that we earnestly seek—or . . . we won't get it, if we grow indifferent. The question of *amnesty* for the Vietnam war resisters illustrates the tension between justice and mercy which is troubling our society today. I should like to turn to Sacred Scripture for some insight toward a solution of this problem. But, before I do, I think it is necessary to point out that there are *three* possible motivations for the granting of an amnesty. First, we may believe that the war resisters were morally wrong, that their actions encouraged the North Vietnamese and thus prolonged the war, increasing the loss of life on both sides, but that by means of an amnesty we should *forgive* them. Secondly, we may believe that the war resisters were morally right, that the war *had* gone on for nearly a decade and might have continued much longer were it not for their dissent, and hence by means of an amnesty we should exonerate them. Or thirdly, we may not make a judgment about the war resisters, refraining from either condemning *or* condoning them, but simply repatriating them, bringing them back, *forgetting* about the guilt or innocence aspect. This is literally the meaning of the word *amnesty:* that is, "forgetfulness", or "oblivion."

For purposes of reflecting on the problem in the light of Scripture, I will be dealing at various points in my scriptural examples with one or another of these three motivations to see if there might be a theological basis for amnesty. Before I start, I'll give you my own personal opinion, as a former political science instructor and a current Christian morals instructor, and that is that the war resisters were in fact morally correct. . . . But I will go on to give you a preview of my ultimate conclusion, which is, that we should avoid judgment on the morality of the war resisters' actions and follow the third motivation for amnesty: namely, that we take amnesty in its literal sense and not make a judgment one way or the other, but simply put the Vietnam war behind us and be reconciled to one another. Now, what does the Bible have to say about all this?

Let's look first at the Old Testament. We usually think of Old Testament morality as very harsh: "An eye for an eye and a tooth for a tooth." In fact, however, when we take the Old Testament as a whole and don't just draw out one-liners like the one I just quoted, we see that mercy is one of the most prominent features of the Old Testament. Beginning on the first pages of the Bible, where humankind messes up God's gift of life by sinning, we see the gracious mercy of God offering man another chance. As often as man sins—and according to salvation history, that's pretty often! —God calls him back again. . . . God is not only a *giving* God, He is a *forgiving* God. And He tells us in the Jewish law, in what Jesus was later to join to love of God as the greatest commandment, that we must be giving and forgiving too. This is the way it's stated in the Book of Leviticus: "You shall not hate your brother in your heart, but you shall reason with your neighbor, lest you bear sin because of him. *You shall not take vengeance or bear any grudge against the sons of your own people,* but you shall love your neighbor as yourself," (Leviticus 19:17-18). The reading about the cities of refuge from the book of Joshua (20:1-6) reminds us of God's instruction that those who have killed through accident should be allowed a place of refuge and then free return to their homeland. Of course the question before us today does not concern those who *killed* without premeditation, but rather those who, *with* premeditation, *refused* to kill. The cases are not the same, certainly, but I suggest that there may be a parallel. How God provided for the solution of this case in the Bible may provide a clue for the solution of our amnesty problem today.

The illustration of God's mercy and loving faithfulness to His people, despite *their* unfaithfulness, is spread upon almost every page of the Old Testament. But it is even more abundantly evident in the New Testament. It is in the New Testament that Jesus gives us the most amazing revelation from God. Namely, that God is a *community*. God is *three* persons in one being: Father, Son, and Holy Spirit. St. John defines this unity in community with one word: *love*. The first letter of John says quite simply: "God is love" (1 John 4:8). Jesus came to tell us that if we are to live the life of God, if we are to have the spirit of God in us, we must be *loving* people. To quote a little more from the first letter of John: "Beloved, let us love one another; for love is of God, and he who loves is born of God and knows God. He who does not love does not know God; for God is love" (1 John 4:7-8).

But of course this leads us to ask the same question that the lawyer asked upon hearing the command of love from Jesus, and that is: "Who *is* my neighbor?" (Luke 10:29). It's not without relevance to our topic to note that the person that Jesus described as neighbor in his parable-answer was a Samaritan . . . one who had broken off from the land of Israel and who adopted an alternate form of the Jewish religion. He was a dissenter, yes, even a *resister* as far as the Jews were concerned. They hated him. And *he* was the person that Jesus chose to exemplify the idea of neighbor!

In making mention of a parable, I would like to point out that Jesus gave neither specific commands nor ready answers for problems. The Gospel records Him as giving only one directive, and that is to love. Beyond that He simply told stories. The parables of Jesus are meant to show the *quality* of love that He asks of us.

Let's take a brief look at two of them. First, the parable of the laborers in the vineyard. The householder in the parable represents God. He sends people out to work at the first hour, promising to give them a denarius. *Later* he sends other people out into the vineyard, promising to give them "what is right." Finally, *at the eleventh hour,* he goes out and finds some men still standing idle and he sends these in too. When it comes time to settle accounts, *he treats all of them the same!* They all get a denarius. And those who had been working all day long started to grumble. They said it *wasn't fair!* They said they had borne the heat of the day and here these malingerers came in after the real work was done and they were rewarded the same as the people who had responded to the original call!

And what does Jesus say? I think the reply He has the householder give is really instructive for our handling of the amnesty question. He says to the one who bore the heat of the day: "Friend, I do *you* no wrong. I choose to give this last person as much as I give you. Am I not allowed to do what I choose with what belongs to me? Or do you begrudge me my generosity?" Translated into present terms, the teaching of Jesus seems to say that magnanimity to the war resisters would not be unfair to those who served. The question before us, then, is whether we care to make God's logic our own.

I might remark in passing, that this fairness consideration can cut both ways. Russell Baker, a columnist for the New York *Times,* has suggested that it was really the American public who dodged the war issue, sending its young men off to fight and die and, to this day, not being able to tell them what it was all about. It is perhaps kinder to us all if we do not try to enter into judgment now.

I'd like to consider now the parable of the prodigal son, or, as I think it should be better named, the parable of the forgiving father. The younger son in the story took his part of the inheritance and went off to a faraway country. And after a while, the memory of his homeland and his father's house awakened in him the desire to return. So he started back, thinking of the words he would say to ask for readmission to the family. He really didn't get a chance to get halfway through what he had decided to say. The father, who represents God the Father in the parable, ran out to meet the son before he had even gotten back home. There was no knocking at the door or begging to come in necessary by the son. The father threw his arms around the son and invested him with all the signs of full membership in the household: the ring, the shoes, the robe. Then he decreed a feast to celebrate the return.

Now comes the most interesting part of the story, the

other brother, the *older* one, comes along. When he finds out what's happened he is upset. He won't go in. Now *he* refuses to be part of the family. The father comes out to him and the elder son says: "These many years I have served you, *and I never disobeyed your command.* But when this *son of yours* came, who has devoured your living with harlots, you killed for him the fatted calf." The father responds: "Son, you are always with me, and all that is mine is yours. But it was fitting to make merry and be glad, for this *'your brother'*—not *'that son of yours'* but *'your brother'* —was dead and is alive; he was lost and is found."

This parable, as the former one, tells us that reconciliation for God isn't based on strict justice, but rather on generosity.

Now I'd like to look briefly at *Paul's* teaching, in his letter to the Ephesians (4:30-5:2). He asks us not to grieve the Holy Spirit—God's spirit in us. He says: Don't be unfaithful to it. He asks us to put all bitterness and wrath and anger and clamor and malice away from us. He asks us to be tenderhearted and forgiving, as God has forgiven us. We are called upon to be imitators of God. We have to *pass along* forgiveness. Thus in the Lord's Prayer we pray: "Forgive us *our* trespasses, *as we forgive* those who trespass against us." I submit that that's a very *risky prayer* for someone to say who takes a hard line on amnesty!

Permit me to return, now to one final quote from the Gospel (Luke 6:36-8). Jesus says: "Be merciful, even as your Father is merciful. Judge not, and you will not be judged; condemn not, and you will not be condemned; forgive, and you will be forgiven. . . . The measure you give will be the measure you get back."

It is perhaps thoughts such as these that inspired the late Richard Cardinal Cushing to ask the following question in his last Easter message: "Would it be too much to ask that we empty our jails of all the protesters—the guilty and the innocent—without judging them, call back over the border and around the world the young men called 'deserters,' drop the cases that are still awaiting judgment on our college youth? . . . Could we not do all this in the name of life, and with life, hope?"

The Cardinal puts that as a *question*—and that is the way it must be treated, as a question put to each of us.

I personally believe that it would not be too much to ask because I believe that we as a nation currently need reconciliation more than we need vindictive prosecution of illegal activity.

The best conclusion to these remarks might well be a prayer. The one I choose is attributed to a man from several hundred years ago named Francis of Assisi. I hope it comes more and more to express a majority sentiment:

> Lord, make us instruments of your peace. Where there is hatred, let us show love. Where there is injury, pardon. Where there is doubt, faith. Where there is despair, hope. Where there is darkness, light. And where there is sadness, joy. Divine Master, grant that we may not so much seek to be consoled as to console; to be understood as to understand; to be loved as to love. For it is in giving that we receive. It is in *pardoning* that *we* are pardoned. And it is in dying that we are born to eternal life. Amen.

THE VICE PRESIDENCY

THE NOMINATION OF GERALD R. FORD [1]

Speaking before a Democratic party conference on October 12, 1973, Senate Majority Leader Mike Mansfield of Montana said that "filling the vacancy caused by the resignation of former Vice President Agnew . . . is a unique experience for the Senate and the Congress . . . another added situation placed on many others which have confronted this country this year." Agnew had resigned on October 10, and House Minority Leader Gerald R. Ford of Michigan was ultimately named by President Nixon to be the new Vice President and confirmed by both houses of Congress. It is the historic uniqueness of this confirmation that calls for the inclusion of two of the speeches associated with the event.

The first speech is by Senator Gaylord A. Nelson (Democrat, Wisconsin), who opposed the nomination because he did not believe that Ford could "provide the kind of inspirational leadership this nation will need should he succeed to the presidency." Although the votes for confirmation in the Senate (92 yeas and 3 nays) and in the House (387 yeas and 35 nays) overwhelmingly supported Ford, Nelson expressed a concern shared by others in Washington and across the country.

The second speech is by Senator Charles H. Percy (Republican, Illinois), who supported the nomination despite a belief that Ford was unlikely "to go down in the annals of history like such great former Vice Presidents as John Adams, Thomas Jefferson, John C. Calhoun, and Theodore Roosevelt." Although in the past Ford and Percy—a liberal Republican—had not always shared similar views on important issues, the Senator concluded by saying that "from the standpoint of morality, ethics, and the fine characteristics we personally know Jerry Ford possesses, we have no hesitancy whatsoever in saying that he will restore to the Office of the Vice President the integrity which recent events have severely damaged."

[1] Speeches delivered in the United States Senate, Washington, D.C., November 27, 1973. Recorded in the *Congressional Record,* November 27, 1973.

Against the Nomination of Gerald R. Ford

GAYLORD A. NELSON [2]

Mr. President, I am casting my vote against confirmation of Mr. Ford because my philosophical differences with him are too fundamental to compromise, and because I do not believe he can provide the kind of inspirational leadership this nation will need should he succeed to the presidency. We are, after all, selecting a potential President. That is what the vice presidency is all about.

On the most important issues of the past decade, including human and civil rights and the war in Vietnam, our respective positions have been fundamentally and irreconcilably at odds. Our differences are of such significance that I cannot support his nomination just as in other circumstances he would not be able to support mine.

This is not an ordinary appointment. It requires confirmation by both houses of Congress. We are not acting on a cabinet appointment which is a peculiarly personal appointment by the President of a personal adviser and consultant who serves at the pleasure of the President. On this appointment we are acting in a unique capacity as electors in behalf of 200 million American people. I regret that I cannot cast an affirmative vote. I do not believe this appointment measures up to the critical demands of the current circumstances faced by the nation.

I intend nothing I have said to be interpreted as a reflection upon Mr. Ford's character or his leadership qualifications within the congressional environment. He is properly respected as an honest and honorable Member of Congress.

[2] For biographical note, see Appendix.

For the Nomination of Gerald R. Ford

Charles H. Percy [3]

Mr. President, it would be a grave mistake for the nation to feel that the Senate takes lightly the responsibility for advising and consenting to the nomination of Gerald Ford to be Vice President of the United States or that we consider it to be such a minor matter that we allocate less than one hour of debate to the issue. The nation should not overlook the fact that exhaustive hearings have been held, by the Committee on Rules and Administration in which the Senate has great confidence. In addition, the members of the Senate are drawing on the experience and knowledge that many of them have had personally in knowing the nominee over a period of many years and on thorough FBI reports.

I am certain also that the leadership—the managers of the present confirmation proceedings—would have provided any amount of time the Senate desired for debate on this particular issue. The very fact that those who have said they intend to vote against the nomination have given their statements in a relatively few minutes, indicates that even they, in their opposition, are doing so from the standpoint of principle rather than out of any questions concerning the nominee's integrity or character or demonstrative ability as a valued leader of Congress.

Mr. President, let me simply state that many of us are under no illusion that we are advising and consenting to someone of the stature of a Founding Father. Indeed, there are few to be found in the country today. We do not think it is a name that will likely go down in the annals of history, like such great former Vice Presidents as John Adams, Thomas Jefferson, John C. Calhoun, and Theodore Roosevelt. But, I think that if we consider, for example, Harry

[3] For biographical note, see Appendix.

Truman, few in the Senate at the moment their colleague, Harry Truman, was nominated to be Vice President or assumed the Office, would have recognized or realized that Harry Truman was capable of the greatness that he achieved as President. I believe that Jerry Ford would be the first to say that though he probably would not yet be classified as one of the potential "great" Vice Presidents, he nonetheless will strive to achieve this stature.

Mr. President, we are substituting our combined judgment, as 535 members of Congress, for months of campaigning, the convention process, and the votes of seventy million people.

It is an awesome responsibility that we assume. We will be casting our votes today, realizing the insight in the words of the first Vice President of the United States, John Adams, who philosophized about his job, saying: "In this job, I am nothing, but I may become everything."

Mr. President, there is probably not a single member of this body who will not have in his mind at the moment he casts his vote today the fact that there is a distinct possibility Jerry Ford could become, through a series of circumstances, "everything" so far as the Government of the United States of America is concerned—at least, in the executive branch of the Government. It is an awesome responsibility we have, to weigh and to search our consciences for the best judgment we can bring forth.

We are aware, also, that the Vice President is more than the oft-quoted "one heartbeat away" from the highest office in the land. We have come to see the Vice President as a molder of public opinion, an effective spokesman for our nation around the world and certainly a proponent of domestic policies which will be extremely important.

It is with these criteria that we evaluate Jerry Ford, his capabilities and his competence.

I feel that he will admirably fulfill these functions. Everything I have seen to date indicates it. Certainly he can be the eyes and ears of the President as he serves in the second highest office in the land. But, we all know that he can do a far better job of being the eyes and ears, the sense and the antennae, of Congress as a whole, and have a profound impact on its input into the presidency.

The President wisely selected Jerry Ford with the thought in mind that Jerry Ford would not be silent concerning his strongly felt convictions about what is right for our country and what is the right course of action for the executive branch to follow.

Mr. President, we are living in unprecedented times. For the first time in our nation's history, we will utilize the Twenty-fifth Amendment to the Constitution which calls upon the President to nominate a new Vice President in case of a vacancy in the office. For the first time in our history a Vice President was forced to resign from office. It was a confidence-shattering experience for the American people.

For these reasons, Mr. President, I want to commend President Nixon on his selection of Gerald Ford as the vice presidential nominee. He will be responsive to the American people's feelings and needs. He will restore integrity and confidence to the second highest office in the land.

Mr. President, when I first met Jerry Ford a quarter of a century ago, he had already been elected to Congress for his first term, and I was in my first year as president of Bell & Howell. We were gathered in Peoria, Illinois, where he was to receive the Junior Chamber of Commerce's award as "One of the Ten Outstanding Young Men in the Nation." I was impressed with Jerry Ford's gracious open manner and his straightforwardness. I have continued to be even more impressed over the years as I have seen him work.

Even as he has risen through the ranks in the House of Representatives and his scope of interest has naturally broadened, Jerry Ford has not lost sight of his first obligation—representing the people of the Fifth Congressional District of Michigan. Even as he became a national leader of the Republican party, he never failed to put the views of his constituents before any other consideration.

Jerry Ford is a man of character and integrity. I am confident that he will take to heart the views of all Americans as easily and sincerely as he has the views of the people he represents in Michigan. I believe he will be as responsive to all Americans as he has been to the people of Michigan.

It was imperative that the Senate Rules Committee investigate Representative Ford's background closely. The American people deserved that and Jerry Ford deserved a thorough investigation so that any questions of misconduct might be dispelled before he assumed high office.

I was impressed with his performance before the committee. His candor and sincerity during the questioning only furthered my notion of what a good Vice President he will be. I believe that all Americans were reassured when, asked to define his concept of the presidency, Congressman Ford replied:

> I think the President has to be a person of great truth, and the American people have to believe that he is truthful. I think that the President has to lead by example, displaying the standards, morally, ethically and otherwise, by which most Americans live their lives.

I expect that Jerry Ford, in his capacity as Vice President, will live up to the high standards he sets for the presidency. He will, I expect be all that the American people would hope their Vice President would be.

Mr. President, in summary, let me say that from the standpoint of morality, ethics, and the fine characteristics we personally know Jerry Ford possesses, we have no hesitancy whatsoever in saying that he will restore to the Office of the Vice President the integrity which recent events have severely damaged, and which I trust will be fully restored by this confirmation process.

ACCEPTANCE SPEECH [4]

GERALD R. FORD [5]

Gerald R. Ford was sworn in as Vice President of the United States on December 6, 1973, immediately following Senate and House confirmation of his nomination. Chief Justice Warren Burger administered the oath of office before a joint session of Congress assembled in the chamber of the House of Representatives.

Vice President Ford's acceptance is a simple speech characteristic of his usual approach to the public. In saying that he was "a Ford, not a Lincoln," he perhaps relieved the tension of the moment, but some may think the punning remark inappropriate. His voice has been described as having a "flat and earnest tone" (John Osborne, *New Republic,* February 23, 1974), his reading as "passionless . . . in a monotone" (Marjorie Hunter, New York *Times,* February 23, 1974), and his delivery as "wooden" (Richard L. Madden, New York *Times,* February 15, 1974).

Mr. President, Mr. Speaker, Mr. Chief Justice, Mr. President Pro Tempore, distinguished guests, and friends: Together we have made history here today. For the first time we have carried out the commands of the Twenty-fifth Amendment.

In exactly eight weeks we have demonstrated to the world that our great republic stands solid, stands strong upon the bedrock of the Constitution.

I'm a Ford, not a Lincoln.

My addresses will never be as eloquent as Mr. Lincoln's. But I will do my very best to equal his brevity and his plain speaking.

I'm deeply grateful to you, Mr. President, for the trust and the confidence your nomination implied.

[4] Delivered to a joint session of Congress in the chamber of the House of Representatives, Washington, D.C., December 6, 1973. Transcript recorded by the New York *Times*.

[5] For biographical note, see Appendix.

As I have throughout my public service under six Administrations, I will try to set a high example of respect for the crushing and lonely burdens which the nation lays upon the President of the United States.

Mr. President, you have my support and my loyalty.

To the Congress assembled, my former colleagues who have elected me on behalf of our fellow countrymen, I express my heartfelt thanks.

As a man of the Congress, let me reaffirm my conviction that the collective wisdom of our two great legislative bodies while not infallible will in the end serve the people faithfully and very, very well.

I will not forget the people of Michigan who sent me to this chamber; or the friends that I have found here.

Mr. Speaker, I understand that the United States Senate intends in a very few minutes to bind me by its rules. For their presiding officer, this amounts practically to a vow of silence.

Mr. Speaker, you know how difficult this is going to be for me. Before I go from this house, which has been my home for a quarter century, I must say I am forever in its debt.

And particularly, Mr. Speaker, thank you, for your friendship which I certainly am not leaving. To you, Mr. Speaker, and to all of my friends here, however you voted an hour ago, I say a very fond goodbye. May God bless the House of Representatives and guide all of you in the days ahead.

Mr. Chief Justice, may I thank you personally for administering the oath.

And thank each of the honorable Justices for honoring me with your attendance.

I pledge to you, as I did the day I was first admitted to the bar, my dedication to the rule of law and equal justice for all Americans.

For standing by my side, as she always has, there are no words to tell you, my dear wife and mother of our four wonderful children, how much their being here means to me.

As I look into the faces that fill this familiar room; and as I imagine those faces in other rooms across the land, I do not see members of the legislative branch, or the executive branch, of the judicial branch—though I am very much aware of the importance of keeping the separate but coequal branches of our Federal Government in balance—I do not see Senators or Representatives, nor do I see Republicans or Democrats, vital as the two-party system is to sustain freedom and responsible government.

At this moment of visible and living unity, I see only Americans. I see Americans who love their country. Americans who work and sacrifice for their country and their children. I see Americans who pray without ceasing for peace among all nations and for harmony at home.

I see new generations of concerned and courageous Americans—but the same kind of Americans; the children and grandchildren of those Americans who met the challenge of December 7—just thirty-two years ago.

Mr. Speaker, I like what I see.

Mr. Speaker I am not discouraged. I am indeed humble to be the fortieth Vice President of the United States. But I am proud, very proud to be one of 200 million Americans.

I promise, my fellow citizens, only this: to uphold the Constitution, to do what is right as God gives me to see the right and within the limited powers and duties of the vice presidency to do the very best that I can for America.

I will do these things with all the strength and good sense that I have and with your help and through your prayers.

Thank you.

APPENDIX

BIOGRAPHICAL NOTES

AIKEN, GEORGE D. (1892–). Born, Dummerston, Vermont; graduate, Brattleboro (Vt.) High School, 1909; lists occupation as farmer; member, Vermont House of Representatives, 1931–35; speaker, 1933–35; lieutenant governor, Vermont, 1935–37; governor, 1937–40; member, US Senate (Republican, Vermont), 1940– ; recipient, numerous service awards for contributions to agricultural and rural life; author, *Pioneering With Wildflowers,* 1933; *Pioneering With Fruits and Berries,* 1936; *Speaking From Vermont,* 1938. (See also *Current Biography: June 1947.*)

BARGER, ROBERT NEWTON (1938–). Born, Peoria, Illinois; B.A., St. Paul Seminary, 1961; M.A., 1965; M.A.T., College of St. Thomas, 1965; Extension Course Institute, USAF, Air University, 1966–68; attended University of Iowa, University of Illinois; special Associated Press correspondent in the Antarctic, 1956–57; staff priest, Newman Foundation, University of Illinois; visiting chaplain, US Congress; participant, Aviation Cadet International Exchange Program, Denmark, 1956; International Geophysical Year Support Program; author, *Amnesty: What Does It Really Mean?,* 1974.

BROOKE, EDWARD W. (1919–). Born, Washington, D.C.; B.S., Howard University, 1941; LL.B., Boston University Law School, 1948; LL.M., 1949; twenty-three honorary degrees; admitted, Massachusetts bar, 1948; private law practice, Roxbury, Massachusetts, 1948–63; attorney general, Massachusetts, 1963–66; member, US Senate (Republican, Massachusetts), 1967– ; US Army, captain, infantry, World War II; recipient, Bronze Star, Combat Infantryman's Badge. (See also *Current Biography: April 1967.*)

COX, ARCHIBALD (1912–). Born, Plainfield, New Jersey; B.A., Harvard, 1934; LL.B., magna cum laude, 1937; LL.D., Loyola University, 1964; LL.D., University of Cincinnati, 1967; admitted, Massachusetts bar, 1937; private law practice, Ropes, Gray, Best, Coolidge & Rugg, Boston, 1938–41; attorney, solicitor general's office, US Department of Justice, 1941–43; associate solicitor, US Department of Labor, 1943–45; lecturer, Harvard Law School, 1945–46; professor of law, 1946–61; Williston professor of law, 1965– ; solicitor general, US Department of Justice, 1961–65; special Watergate prosecutor, 1973; author, *Law and the National Labor Policy,* 1960; *Civil Rights, the Constitution and the Courts* (with Mark DeWolfe Howe and J. R. Wiggins), 1967; *The Warren Court,* 1968; *Cases on Labor Law* (with Derek C. Bok), 1969. (See also *Current Biography: July 1961.*)

FORD, GERALD R. (1913–). Born, Omaha, Nebraska; B.A., University of Michigan, 1935, LL.B., Yale Law School, 1941; seven honorary doctorates; admitted, Michigan bar, 1941; private law practice, Grand Rapids, Michigan, 1941–49; member, US House of Representatives (Republican, Michigan), 1949–73; minority leader, 1965–73; confirmed as Vice President of the United States by Senate and House of Representatives, December 6, 1973; USN, 1942–46. (See also *Current Biography: March 1961.*)

GALLAGHER, WES (1911–). Born, San Francisco, California; B.A., Louisiana State University, 1935; reporter, Baton Rouge *State Times,* 1935; Rochester *Democrat and Chronicle,* 1935–36; employee, Associated Press, 1937– ; foreign correspondent, twenty-six countries, 1940–51; general executive, New York City, 1951–54; assistant general manager, 1954–62; general manager, 1962– ; president, 1972– ; recipient, William Allen White Award, 1967; John Peter Zenger Award of University of Arizona, 1968; Carvan Anda Award of Ohio University, 1969; George Polk Award of Long Island University, 1969; author, *Back Door to Berlin,* 1943.

GOODMAN, STANLEY J. (1910–). Born, Montreal, Canada; B.A., McGill University, 1931; M.A., 1932; M.B.A., Harvard University, 1934; arrived, United States, 1932; naturalized, 1940; employee, Arco Company, Cleveland, 1934–36; C.I.T. Financial Corporation, 1936–42; Interstate Department Stores, 1942–48; May Department Stores Company, St. Louis, 1948– ; vice president, 1958–66; president, 1967– ; chief executive officer, 1969– ; chairman of the board, 1972– ; director, trustee, numerous business and civic organizations and programs; articles, *Harper's Magazine, Harvard Business Review.*

HATFIELD, MARK O. (1922–). Born, Dallas, Oregon; B.A., Willamette University, 1943; M.A., Stanford University, 1948; numerous honorary degrees; resident assistant, Stanford University, 1947–49; instructor, political science, Willamette University, 1949; dean of students, associate professor, 1950–56; member, Oregon House of Representatives, 1951–55; member, Oregon Senate, 1955–57; secretary of state, Oregon, 1957–59; governor, 1959–67; member, US Senate (Republican, Oregon), 1967– ; USNR, 1943–46. (See also *Current Biography: November 1959.*)

JEFFREY, ROBERT C. (1927–). Born, San Antonio, Texas; B.A., University of Iowa, 1949; M.A., 1950; Ph.D., 1957; assistant professor, Cornell College, 1950–53; instructor, University of Iowa, 1953–54; assistant professor, University of Virginia,

1954–59; associate professor, Indiana University, 1959–68; professor, chairman, Department of Speech Communication, University of Texas, 1968– ; executive secretary, Speech Association of America, 1960–63; president, Speech Communication Association, 1973; author, *Legislative Procedures in the General Assembly of the State of Indiana* (with George W. Meyers), 1969; *Speech: A Text With Adapted Readings* (with Owen Peterson), 1971.

KISSINGER, HENRY A. (1923–). Born, Fürth, Germany; B.A., summa cum laude, Harvard, 1950; M.A., 1952; Ph.D., 1954; Phi Beta Kappa; arrived, United States, 1938; naturalized, 1943; executive director, Harvard International Seminar, 1951–60; lecturer, government, Harvard University, 1957–59; associate professor, 1959–62; professor, 1962–69; director, special studies project, Rockefeller Brothers Fund, Inc., 1956–59; consultant to Presidents Eisenhower, Kennedy, Johnson; assistant to President Nixon, national security affairs, 1969– ; secretary, US Department of State, 1973– ; US Army, 1943–46; recipient, Bronze Star; author, *Nuclear Weapons and Foreign Policy,* 1957; *A World Restored,* 1957; *The Necessity For Choice: Prospects of American Foreign Policy,* 1961; *The Troubled Partnership: A Reappraisal of the Atlantic Alliance,* 1965; *American Foreign Policy: Three Essays,* 1969; over forty articles in various journals. (See also *Current Biography: June 1972.*)

MEAD, MARGARET (1901–). Born, Philadelphia, Pennsylvania; B.A., Barnard College, 1923; M.A., Columbia University, 1924; Ph.D., 1929; Phi Beta Kappa; twenty honorary doctorates, honorary Doctor of Science, Harvard University, 1973; assistant curator of ethnology, American Museum of Natural History, 1926–42; associate curator, 1942–64; curator, 1964–69; curator emeritus, 1969– ; adjutant professor, anthropology, Columbia University, 1954– ; chairman, Social Science Division, Fordham University, 1968–71; professor, 1969–71; recipient, American Museum of Natural History Gold Medal, 1969; president, Scientists' Institute for Public Information, American Anthropological Association, World Federation for Mental Health; president, secretary, Society for Applied Anthropology; vice president, New York Academy of Sciences; member, executive board, American Association for the Advancement of Science; New Guinea expeditions, 1931–33, 1938, 1953, 1964, 1965, 1967, 1971; Bali expeditions, 1936–38, 1957–58; author, *Rap on Race* (with James Baldwin), 1971; *Twentieth Century Faith: Hope and Survival,* 1972; *Blackberry Winter: My Earlier Years,* 1972; and numerous other works. (See also *Current Biography: May 1951.*)

MOOS, MALCOLM C. (1916–). Born, St. Paul, Minnesota; B.S., University of Minnesota, 1937; M.A., 1938; Ph.D., University of California, 1942; honorary degrees, Ohio Northern University, University of North Dakota, Georgetown University, Johns Hopkins University, College of Saint Thomas, University of Notre Dame; assistant professor, political science, University of Wisconsin, 1942; assistant professor, Johns Hopkins University, 1942–46; associate professor, 1946–52; professor, 1952–61, 1963; associate editor, Baltimore *Evening Sun,* 1945–48; visiting professor, University of Michigan, 1955; consultant, White House, 1957–58; administrative assistant to President Eisenhower, 1958–61; adviser to Rockefeller Brothers Fund, Inc., 1961–63; professor, public law and government, Columbia University, 1963–65; director, policy and planning, Ford Foundation, 1964–66; director, Office of Government and Law, Ford Foundation, 1966–67; president, University of Minnesota, 1967–74; director, Center for the Study of Democratic Institutions, 1974– ; director, member, consultant, numerous committees, boards, and commissions; author, *A Grammar of American Politics: The National, State, and Local Governments* (with W. E. Binkley), 1949; *Politics, Presidents, and Coattails,* 1952; *Power Through Purpose: The Realism of Idealism as a Basis for Foreign Policy* (with Thomas I. Cook), 1955; *The Republicans: A History of Their Party,* 1956. (See also *Current Biography: November 1968.*)

NELSON, GAYLORD A. (1916–). Born, Clear Lake, Wisconsin; B.A., San Jose State College, 1939; LL.B., University of Wisconsin Law School, 1942; admitted, Wisconsin Bar, 1942; private law practice, Madison, Wisconsin, 1946–59; member, Wisconsin Senate, 1949–58; governor, 1959–62; member, US Senate (Democrat, Wisconsin), 1963– ; US Army, World War II. (See also *Current Biography: May 1960.*)

NIXON, RICHARD M. (1913–). Born, Yorba Linda, California; B.A., Whittier College, 1934; LL.B., Duke University, 1937; private law practice, Whittier, California, 1937–41; attorney, Office of Emergency Management, Washington, D.C., 1942; member, US House of Representatives (Republican, California), 1947–51; member, US Senate, 1951–53; Vice President of the United States, 1953–61; unsuccessful Republican candidate for President, 1960; resumed law practice, Los Angeles, 1961–63; New York, 1963–68; elected President of the United States, 1968; reelected 1972; USN, lieutenant commander, 1942–46; author, *Six Crises,* 1962. (See also *Current Biography: December 1969.*)

PERCY, CHARLES H. (1919–). Born, Pensacola, Florida; B.A., University of Chicago, 1941; eight honorary degrees; employee, Bell & Howell, 1936–66; president, 1949–61; chairman of the board, 1961–66; member, US Senate (Republican, Illinois), 1967– ; officer, trustee, numerous organizations; recipient, many awards; decorated officer, French Legion of Honor; elected one of Ten Outstanding Young Men of 1949, US Junior Chamber of Commerce; USNR, lieutenant, 1943–45. (See also *Current Biography: December 1959.*)

RICHARDSON, ELLIOT L. (1920–). Born, Boston, Massachusetts; B.A., cum laude, Harvard, 1941; LL.B., cum laude, 1947; clerk for Judge Learned Hand, US Court of Appeals, 1947–48; clerk for Justice Felix Frankfurter, US Supreme Court, 1948–49; private law practice, Ropes, Gray, Best, Coolidge & Rugg, Boston, 1949–53; 54–57; lecturer, Harvard Law School, 1952; assistant to Senator Leverett Saltonstall, 1953–54; assistant secretary for legislation, US Department of Health, Education, and Welfare, 1957–59; US attorney for Massachusetts, 1959–61; partner, Ropes and Gray, 1961–64; lieutenant governor, Massachusetts, 1965–67; attorney general, 1967–69; under secretary, US Department of State, 1969–70; secretary, US Department of Health, Education, and Welfare, 1970–73; secretary, US Department of Defense, 1973; attorney general, US Department of Justice, 1973; US Army, World War II. (See also *Current Biography: March 1971.*)

SARGENT, FRANCIS W. (1915–). Born, Hamilton, Massachusetts; graduate, Massachusetts Institute of Technology, 1939; owner, Goose Hummock Shop, Inc.; chairman, Atlantic States Marine Fisheries Commission, 1956–59; chairman, Massachusetts Water Resources Commission, 1956–59; commissioner, Massachusetts Department of Public Works, 1965–66; lieutenant governor, Massachusetts, 1967–69; governor, 1969– ; US Army, World War II; recipient, Bronze Star, Purple Heart with oak leaf cluster. (See also *Current Biography: June 1971.*)

WEICKER, LOWELL P., JR. (1931–). Born, Paris, France; B.A., Yale University, 1953; LL.B., University of Virginia School of Law, 1958; admitted, Connecticut bar, 1960; private law practice, several years; member, Connecticut State Assembly, 1963–69; member, US House of Representatives (Republican, Connecticut), 1969–71; member, US Senate, 1971– ; US Army, 1953–55; US Army Reserve, 1959–64. (See also *Current Biography: January 1974.*)

CUMULATIVE AUTHOR INDEX

1970-1971—1973-1974

A cumulative author index to the volumes of REPRESENTATIVE AMERICAN SPEECHES for the years 1937-1938 through 1959-1960 appears in the 1959-1960 volume and for the years 1960-1961 through 1969-1970 in the 1969-1970 volume.

(6811)